Training the Mind of your Gun Dog

Training the Mind of your Gun Dog

J.A. Kersley and F. Haworth

Illustrated by James Croft

London
PELHAM BOOKS

First published in Great Britain by Pelham Books Ltd
52 Bedford Square, London WC1B 3EF
1977

ISBN 0 7207 0948 2

Set and printed in Great Britain by
Tonbridge Printers Ltd, Peach Hall Works, Tonbridge, Kent
in Plantin eleven on thirteen point on paper supplied by
P. F. Bingham Ltd, and bound by Redwood Burn
at Esher, Surrey

Cover picture: 'Gaythorne Feather', owned by Jack
Thornton, photographed by Nora Thornton.

To that happy company
who believe that a hound, a horse, a hawk or a
man should be allowed to pursue their natural
instincts in the countryside which is their true
heritage.

'In the first place, let us consider the nature of dogs in general, wherein they agree, and their common properties of nature, such as are not destroyed in the distinction of kind but remain like infallible truths and invariable in every kind and country throughout the world.

'There is not any creature more irrational, more loving to her master, nor more serviceable than a dog, enduring blows from his hands, and using no other means to pacify his displeasure than humiliation and prostration and after beating, turneth a revenge into a more fervent love. Irrational, did I say?

'Then it is admirable to observe that natural instinct of emnity and cunning, whereby one beast being, as it were, confederate with man, by whom he is maintained, serves him in his design upon others. How perfect is the scent or smell of an hound, who never leaves it, but follows it through innumerable changes and variation of other scents even over and in the water and into the earth.

'For as it is the privilege of Man who is endowed with reason, and authorised in the Law of his Creation to subdue the Beasts of the field, so to tyrannise over them too much is brutish. . . .'

The Gentleman's Recreations,

NICHOLAS COX, 1674

Contents

Preface

In this book we have tried to study the mind of the dog and then used the knowledge in practical training to overcome the difficulties encountered. We have concentrated on faults, because dogs are always developing them and the trainer of dogs is always being asked how to correct them. In the training sections we have taken for granted that the reader has some knowledge of basic training and have omitted the few simple exercises needed to train a dog and exact obedience from him.

The main fascination in dog training arises from the study of the individual personality of each dog, so that although basic training methods are the same they have to be continually modified to suit your particular animal – an exercise or punishment used to correct the fault in one dog will not succeed with another. In the end it is the dog who has the power of decision as to which course of action he wishes to take. So it's up to the trainer to offer sufficient inducements to persuade the dog to take the line the trainer wishes him to take. While a human being will decide on a course of action to be taken by argument, we hope rational, a dog will make a decision according to the relative strength of the urges involved – a dog is unable to be rational but he will follow a leader. His master will question a decision, but the dog, who lives entirely in the present, has no such difficulties – he will obey any order without question provided his basic needs are satisfied and catered for. Punish a dog and he has forgotten it the next moment until it is recalled to his memory by a similar set of circumstances or the scent of his master.

It must never be forgotten that you can put a lot into a dog and arrive at an animal which is quite brilliant at a shoot or on field trials, but this has been achieved by the happy chance of heredity and your training, and principally heredity at that. A

9

dog never produces anything either by constructive action or thought. Such actions as he produces are controlled either by his emotions, while a human being's emotions are controlled by the higher centres of his brain.

The retriever breeds consist of black and yellow and chocolate labradors, flat-coated and curly-coated retrievers, chesapeakes and poodles, and in Ireland and America the Irish water spaniel. It is on these pure retrievers that we have concentrated; however, all gun dogs have the same basic instincts and attitudes of mind, so there is no essential difference in training a labrador or a spaniel. The same exercises are used for both breeds: both breeds have to be steady when out, hunt and retrieve smartly and keep to heel. The spaniel, however, has also to be taught to quarter and to drop to shot, as they have to find and pick up game, but these differences are not great and will be discussed later.

This book has been written so that the shooting man, the amateur dog handler and the novice trainer may get the best out of the dog, not on the principle that by elimination he will possess an animal that is a champion – you possess a dog, this is your dog, and you wish to train him to as high a standard as possible. Most dogs will respond if you understand the particular animal, and as it is not possible for most of us to discard our dog we're stuck with our particular animal however much he may try our patience.

Golden Retriever

Chesapeake

Labrador

Springer Spaniel

Irish Water Spaniel

Cocker Spaniel

Wolf

Some gun dogs and their common ancestor

I

The Dog as a Pack Animal

'Be a good animal, true to your animal instincts'

It's fascinating and not without merit to consider the daily life of the pack animal, which hunts and kills to live. The wolf, the dog's ancestor, is the supreme example: having found a suitable place, the male and female dig out their den, and when the pups arrive the male acts as provider while the female gets on with the job of rearing the family, feeding them by regurgitation. She is a stern mother, growling at them, nipping them and making them squeal, shaking and even throwing them about, and the pups can show fear by rolling on their backs in the submissive attitude. The pups grow up, learning by playing with each other and by chasing anything that moves, from rabbits to butterflies. Later the mother takes the pups out and teaches them individual hunting and what to fear, and still later the mother and father and the pups go out on hunting trips. When they kill, they first eat the offal, and from that get valuable vegetable matter, but in any case they are omnivorous eaters and will consume snails, mice, berries, rabbits or any small beast that comes to hand. On trips the male acts as guard to his family – wolves are generally mono-gamous, an attribute rarely demonstrated in our dogs these days. Even during this period, families may show sociability and perhaps share a den; food is then brought back to the den for all to share. The wolf packs may consist of only a couple of families, or there may be more, but they call to each other, collect together and start to hunt, following a trail over many miles and showing great strength, endurance and perseverance. The pack may split up according to a preconceived plan and, having killed, share the food until each is completely satiated and goes his own way alone and in solitude sleeps off the feast.

A dog is a pack animal – to say this is not enough, it's necessary to investigate what it entails. A pack is usually made up of several family units – it's an extension of the family. Separate individuals trying to join the pack have to be vetted over a period and then are either accepted or rejected. This, of course, occurs in kennels when a newcomer is introduced. All pack animals have certain basic instincts – obviously, to follow one another, but also, not quite so obviously, to lead. If while hunting a pack splits, a leader is chosen for the second pack. In all hound packs there are dogs who do most of the work and the rest follow. Pack animals, therefore, acquire a quality of leadership and independent action. By living in a pack they are gregarious and do not wish to be left on their own; they are also willing to share their food. They can co-operate with each other and prepare ambushes. They, of course, have the basic instincts of pursuing and hunting and they also have the instinct to guard.

In training we build on these basic instincts, habit patterns modifying the instinct to achieve our purpose. We also take an instinct, such as chasing or running in, and deny it to the dog. This is far more difficult to do and as the instinct has been inbred for centuries it is impossible to eliminate it entirely. If we wish to modify an instinct we build up associations (see next chapter) and strengthen the association by praise. If we deny an instinct we have to do it by reprimand

and repression, and continue the firmness until the habit pattern achieved is stronger than the basic instinct.

In a simple seen retrieve the dog denies his instinct to chase until he is sent out. After he has gone out he hunts when his master tells him to do so; this is following his instinct of hunting at a check. Having found the quarry he does not kill, the instinct to kill having been bred out of our labradors over the years. His instinct now is to take the kill off on his own, possibly to his den. But by training we modify this and persuade him to follow another instinct: that is to share it with the other members of the pack and, as he accepts his master as his pack leader, he gives his kill to us. It has been known for a trained retriever to retrieve pigeons and take them back to where his master had left the game bag rather than retrieve them to hand.

Pack animals can communicate instinctively and quite extensively with each other by voice and gesture. A dog, if he wants you or another dog to follow him, will run up to you, then move away and wait, and repeat this until you follow. This power of communication is essential because, after all, we have to communicate extensively with our dogs by sound and gesture and if the dog could not understand us we should fail before we had even begun. A pack animal living in a community has also to show a great capacity for adaptability – dogs are indeed adaptable in every sense of the word. Adaptability is the faculty of accepting changed conditions and learning from them – certainly our dogs have a great capacity for learning and again we should fail if this adaptability were not present in their make-up as a pack animal.

Although all these instincts are present in puppies, they have to be taught and brought out by their parents and other members of the pack so that they conform with pack law and adapt themselves into their particular level in the social system. We are convinced that, although instincts develop automatically as a pup grows up, we can help him by very early training. Some people deny this – as far as the simple instinct is concerned, we agree it is there already, but we are modifying instincts. All young things learn very quickly and what they learn sticks for life. So we should cash in on their quickness in learning and long memory by teaching them at an early date. A child can be moulded for life by his early training, and so can that much more primitive being, a dog.

II

The Mind of a Dog

'On the whole, we are not intelligent!'

The physiologists think of the animal mind as a computer built up of conditioned reflexes. Aunty Mary, on the strength of the true story of the young dog who used to lead an old blind dog around by holding it by the ear, considers dogs intelligent, compassionate and of a high moral calibre. Although the physiologists' argument is valid to a considerable extent, the term 'conditioned reflex' is not going to be used in this context. This term has through misuse acquired the significance of a computer-like brain where information is pushed in and a result spewed out, as long as the programming is correct. Dogs have personalities, urges, desires and to some extent the power of decision.

It is not permissible to project the human mind into that of a dog. It is quite permissible to analyse a dog's mind to see how the relative primitive mind compares and differs from that of his master. All brains are anatomically and physiologically comparable and the human brain must have gone through many stages of development. All brains have to be able to form associations, otherwise they could not function. So we must first define what an association is. An association

17

is the power of linking events and stimuli together in the mind. A definition of an association is that the mind has the capacity of storing impressions, of linking two or more impressions together, and therefore of memory, if you repeat a stimulus a sufficient number of times. When this has happened the dog will remember the result of those stimuli and act accordingly. For example, one associates glass with transparency and hardness. A bird does not make this association and flies into the glass. To form an association, the brain, by definition, has to have memory, otherwise the association could not exist in time, but, as memory fades, an association has to be repeated several times to make it a permanent part of the brain's make-up. If an association leads to action, after a time the action is performed without conscious thought. To hasten this process we endeavour to link the association we are teaching the dog with pleasure or pain in order to make more impression on the dog's brain. A dog likes being praised or patted. Why, it is difficult to know, except that friendly noises are the opposite to fear and reassure a dog that all is well. It is possible to growl at a dog and teach him it is praise and he will wag his tail, then to speak softly to him and teach him it is a reprimand and he will cringe and cower away in fright – both are instances of association. Associations are, therefore, essential for learning.

To teach a dog it is necessary to build on a basic inherited instinct, to modify this instinct by association and produce a habit pattern, to impress and strengthen this habit pattern in the dog's mind by using his emotions. For example, a dog instinctively hunts. Click your fingers while he is hunting and he will associate clicking with hunting, then every time you click your fingers he will start hunting. The habit pattern is impressed on the dog by praise and repetition until it is automatic; then, as memory fades, it must be repeated from time to time to ensure that it has become a permanent part of the dog's make-up. In the wild it would be the hunting cry of the pack leader which would trigger off the dog's hunting pattern.

Now a habit pattern may be elaborated by further association until a very complicated series of events ensues. A shooting dog is taught to hunt and retrieve. This is associated with his master's gun, a journey by car, his master's shooting clothes and even possibly a certain time of the day or day of the week. Dogs have time sense, so on the day his master is going to take him out shooting, he smells his master's clothes, then the gun his master picks up, and he waits in eager excitement for his master to take him out to the car. This series of associations and events is called a 'chain reaction' and the whole complicated series of associations has been built up from the dog's inherited instinct to hunt.

What is an instinct? An instinct is an action or series of actions passed down by heredity which an animal performs without having to learn or be taught, or even think about. It is purely reflex. To deny an instinct is very much more difficult than to encourage and modify it and it is only accomplished by reprimand. However, not only must the dog know what the punishment is about, the punishment must also be made as positive as possible. This is not always easy, but a hard jerk on the check cord – if one is used – or the lead when a dog is walking to heel and runs in front, is a positive form of punishment as it pulls him back, and it is better than a flick with a switch which makes him go down but is entirely negative.

Neurosis

It cannot be disputed that dogs can develop neuroses and that it is easier to cause a neurosis in some dogs than in others. There is a hereditary factor and a temperamental one – wild animals, as far as is known, do not become neurotic, but a kennel dog will. If a dog is over-confined he may react in two ways. He may tear the place to pieces: he is an escapist, showing his frustration and taking positive action, this is not neurosis; or he may start pacing aimlessly on and on – this is neurotic behaviour. Neurosis is brought about by presenting a dog with a problem that he cannot solve. He may get over-excited and hysterical; he may, for example, as one dog did, stand on his hind legs and yip. Or he may go into a corner and sulk and, refusing all action, opt out and forget his training. A dog who cannot solve a problem, knowing he is going to get punished painfully for his failure, develops a neurosis far more quickly than one who is not punished. This is very different from the dog who disobeys because he wants to, and gets punished for his disobedience. The trainer must be able to distinguish the difference.

Brain-washing

It is always extremely irritating when a member of the lay public accuses a trainer of brain-washing his dogs. They do not understand the true nature of the term. Brain-washing consists, in fact, of giving an animal such a severe shock that he is reduced to a state of extreme terror; or of continuous torture, starvation and imprisonment, reducing him to such a state that any mental capacity previously acquired is lost. The animal is then given further things to learn on this blank mind. The original discovery of brain-washing was made by Pavlov with dogs, but was undoubtedly practised on human beings by the Inquisition and in medieval torture chambers. Brain-washing is, in fact, self-defeating, principally because you are trying to build on a zombie – 'For those whom god to ruin has designed he fits for fate and first destroys the mind.'

Emotions

A dog can experience all the emotions that a human can. This is not to be wondered at, because our emotions are situated at a low level and in a primitive part of our brain – emotions are often very low and basic anyhow! We control and sublimate our emotions by our higher centres, or we hope we do. A dog's emotions are not under cerebral control. Humour, for example, is alien to a dog's nature. Humour consists of an emotion: cruelty, happiness or some other emotion which has been elaborated by imagination and abstract thought – a dog cannot be consciously cruel. A man slipping on a banana skin gives exquisite pleasure to the beholder because he has the imagination to visualize the sore bottom which will result from the fall – a dog cannot do this. A dog can, therefore, fear or hate, be angry, jealous, selfish or greedy, can love, be happy or contented, be bored or interested and excited – or any other basic emotion you can think of. When talking of the emotions, the endocrine glands must not be forgotten. A discussion of them has no place in this book except to note that they have a powerful effect on the emotions. We all know that under the influence of the gonads love conquers all, and if satisfied makes the dog masterful and the bitch docile; if thwarted the bitch becomes bitchy and the dog a great nuisance. But other glands also modify, control and trigger off emotional responses.

The effect of pain or fear is very important in training. All pain confuses and extreme fear paralyses and leads to cessation of action. To illustrate this, the rabbit is paralysed by the stoat, the fawn remains still in its form when frightened, we are petrified by fear, which is followed by panic, and panic is mindless confusion. Kipling said: 'If you can keep your head when all about you are losing theirs ... you will be a man.' But we are not talking of men, we are talking of dogs, and fear in a dog gives rise to either cessation of action or a panic to escape – it does not lead to constructive thought. That pain causes confusion is more easily understood. Have you ever tried to do your accounts when you have a toothache – the pain fills the mind – or to talk brightly and intelligently to the girl next door when you have a belly-ache? Your thoughts will be concentrated on your belly and not on her charms. It is, therefore, necessary to use fear and pain very carefully when training, otherwise the result obtained is opposite to the one desired. 'No passion so effectively robs the mind of all its powers of reasoning and acting as fear.'

Intelligence

To what degree is a dog intelligent? First and foremost, what is intelligence? The answer, we suppose, is that it is the ability to work out a problem on one's own by reasoned thought. If this is applied to dogs they show very little real intelligence. The faculty of learning varies in dogs, some are very quick, others are very 'thick' but this is not intelligence, it is only the speed at which the particular dog picks up associations. It is, of course, no use punishing a slow learner as this only confuses him and makes him slower – pain confuses. The only hope a trainer has of teaching a slow learner is to use two high qualities of the human mind, patience and fortitude, under stress. Watch a young dog trying to negotiate a fence. In the beginning he will try to get through absurdly small holes, even though bigger ones are present. If you lift the wire he will not try to take advantage of this and squeeze under. Even though the fence be low he will not try to clamber over it. His attempts to solve this problem are simply trial and error until eventually he stumbles on the right hole or is shown a way over. Once he has built up the association he will continue to use the method he has learnt. However, the dog has realized that a problem exists, so that indicates some intelligence. The solution to the problem, however, has not been achieved by rational thought, he has just blundered about until chance solved it for him. Now if for some reason the method he has learnt by association to solve a problem fails, he is back to Stage 1 and has to find out a further solution by trial and error. A dog cannot argue out a conclusion, nor can he think abstractedly. A dog's thoughts, as he has little language, are scents, visual images and urges. We must, therefore, accept that a dog has a capacity for learning if taught by an intelligent human being. He has a limited capacity for educating himself by trial and error, but he has no true insight or understanding of what it is all about. He will soon learn that rabbits lie in tussocks of grass but not on a plain field – an association – but he will go endlessly out to fetch dummies, which must, after all, to him be a completely useless manoeuvre. A dog told to swim a river will do so, then come back by water. If, however, there is a bridge 50 yards down and he sees it, he will come back by the bridge if he has used a bridge before. Even a hedgehog learns to curl up into a ball and roll down a steep bank as the most comfortable and easy way of reaching the bottom. A dog will use a pedestrian crossing after he has been nearly run over several times and has been taken over it by his master with the cars stopped – another association – or perhaps he is only using his scenting ability and smelling the human tracks. A dog has the intelligence, therefore, to realize that there is a problem, and also the intelligence to persevere in the solution of that problem, so let the little dog work it out for himself by association or chance.

Just occasionally, however, a dog performs some action which appears to show a real intelligence – but these occurrences are very rare and most of them can be explained by association. We have no explanation for the following occurrence.

A very clever dog was sent on a retrieve which entailed a very considerable expenditure of energy and he came back somewhat exhausted to be met by a five-barred gate. The dog pushed the pheasant through the gate, leapt the gate and picked the pheasant up on the other side and then brought it to hand. Watching this retrieve, it certainly appeared that the dog was using his intelligence. However, these occasions are so rare, and actions which appear to be intelligent can so often be explained by association that it is possible that even in this case there was some other explanation – it may have occurred, for instance, by chance on a previous occasion and the dog had remembered.

Imitation

A dog is said not to imitate and this can be demonstrated time and time again if dogs are carefully and critically watched while training. Sometimes if one dog jumps a fence another will follow, but this is not imitation, this is an example of the 'follow' instinct, inherent in a pack animal. Jump a fence, by all means, if you wish to train your dog to jump and he will follow, but heaven help you if he tries to imitate you!

Memory

It has been demonstrated in this chapter that a dog has a good memory, otherwise he could not learn, although the capacity for learning and therefore for memory varies from dog to dog. That he has a superb memory for scents is undoubted – once scented, never forgotten. He also has an extremely good memory for places and minute details of a place he has visited. This is probably true of most animals, certainly of the horse to whom the jockey shows the jumps before he takes him over them before running a race. While training one finds that a dog will try to get through the same gap in the hedge which he has remembered from a previous occasion. This was demonstrated by a well-trained dog when a marked retrieve was thrown forward over the hedge into the next field. The dog, who had not been in that area for a month or two, and then perhaps only on one or two occasions, whipped round, ran back, went through a small gap in the side hedge, then ran forward, and through the side hedge again to collect the retrieve. He had remembered the holes in the hedge. The trainer was curious to see what would happen on this occasion and he let him run on – normally he would have used the stop whistle to guide him through the hedge where he wanted him to go, as a dog has to be taught to face cover. He had, of course, previously seen that it was possible to get through the hedge at this point.

Although, as demonstrated by this incident, a dog has a good memory, if a person or a place is recalled to him by association of sight or scent, he still lives entirely in the present - he has no future because he lacks imagination, and he has very little past. He does not dwell on past sights or even on past happiness. He accepts his lot, and if there is nothing to stimulate him to action he goes to sleep.

Time Sense

All animals have a good sense of time and will lead their daily lives according to a time programme. A dog can be trained to perform at, for example, a three-minute interval with great accuracy. Dogs do, without doubt, know their feeding times, or the time of any other important occurrence in their daily lives. Their lives are also governed by the rhythm of the seasons and by the rhythm of day turning into night and night into day. Migrating birds will start on their long journeys almost to the day provided the winds are favourable, and birds, of course, breed in rotation according to their kind and the season of the year. A dog will know the day of the week if it is important to him, even if there is no particular association to recall it to his memory. In fact, they have a better time sense than we have since we have learned to depend on our wrist-watches and our time instinct has atrophied.

Communication

In our present day we are always complaining of our failure to communicate with each other. Not only have animals succeeded in communicating between themselves with a very high degree of success, but our dogs have succeeded in living and communicating with us. It is our failure that at times we fail to communicate with our dogs, and this is the whole problem of training. Animals communicate with each other by a complicated system of language and gestures, all of which are completely understood among themselves. However, an African crow cannot communicate successfully with an English crow. The successful trainer should learn to communicate with his animals, and if he fails to do this his success will be limited. This is not sentimentality, nor is it elevating an animal to human status – it is practical training. Be severe and firm, but endeavour to remember your limitations at the same time. If only we could learn dog language and gestures and talk to them in their own language, then we would be pack leaders worth following. It would be nice to be like the goose man who really had learnt goose language. When he called they followed him in file, when he reached a field he could tell them to eat, although there was no food there; and when he told them to fly they tried to, although they were tame geese and had never flown in their lives. Do not think this is nonsense. If you can control a dog when he is with you or out hunting by modifications in tone, then you are beginning to communicate with your dog. Some trainers can only train dogs of a certain type. It is agreed that the trainer must have the right type of dog for him and one that he can communicate with. Some trainers prefer bitches, others dogs, some find that they can cope better with the cloven ones rather than with those that are crested!

Adaptability

A further attribute of dogs is that they are highly adaptable. They can keep healthy with very little exercise or cope with a great deal. They can live in a flat or on a farm; they can flourish on a very varied diet. It is interesting to note that wolves can be domesticated because a wolf is a dog. Have you ever tried to domesticate a tiger – or a cow? There would be cow pats in your withdrawing room.

Studying the mind of a dog theoretically is worth while in practical training. Many people who have great success in training dogs acquire their knowledge by practical experience, and gain success even though their methods go contrary to theoretical considerations. They have gained their experience over the years and during the process have possibly spoilt many dogs or not brought out the best in them. They have, in fact, been using a trial and error method, like their dogs.

What are the main points in this chapter?

(1) That pain and fear confuse and paralyse to some degree. This does not mean to suggest that a short, sharp reminder on a disobedient or lazy dog does not work wonders, but it should not be too often repeated. We all have to be reminded from time to time who is boss. As Dr Johnson said: 'Depend upon it, sir, when a man knows he is to be hanged in a fortnight it concentrates his mind wonderfully,' but this, remember, was a fortnight before the execution, not after!

(2) That dogs are not intelligent, and have to be taught by association – which means that the trainer has to solve all their problems for them.

(3) That all training should as far as possible be positive and not negative, and that it is easier to modify an instinct than to deny it.

(4) That a dog has all the emotions and, if training is wrong, a neurotic dog will result – a dog must never be put in a

position where he cannot solve the problem presented to him.

(5) That a dog lives in the present – he has no future and very little past. This means that a dog does not think about or dwell in the past. He has a good memory, so has the power of recall if it is brought to his attention by a definite stimulus, such as scent, or if he visits a place he remembers.

There is no doubt, however, that by training we can improve a dog's memory. We have tried to differentiate in this chapter between a dog's memory and his very limited intelligence.

III

Some Aspects of Scenting

'But soft, methinks I scent the morning air.'

A dog has the scenting ability denied to man in that he can analyse a scent into its various components. A bloodhound or American Coon Hound can follow a 24-hour-old scent, however many people have walked across it and confused it, and follow it for many miles. A dog can differentiate into its several components that mess of potage we call a dog's dinner, so there is no point in giving a dog three courses! And perhaps the dog-meat manufacturers are after all correct when they label the tin of their product which consists of cereal and reconstituted offal 'Liver and Chicken Supreme'. His nose is a delicate computer that not only can smell objects which we do not believe to have any scent at all, like salt, and in great dilution, but can differentiate one scent from another and the relative strength of a specific scent so as to avoid back-tracking when on a trail.

A trained dog will follow a scent, ignoring fresh tracks that have crossed his path and other delightful and interesting odours that come his way. He is rather like a man who has just taken his marriage vows, has sworn to forsake all others and to cleave only to his wedded wife. Of course, there are

29

plenty of backsliders: the young dog who likes to experiment and will follow anything that takes his fancy, and the older dog who has either not matured or who has not been sufficiently disciplined and trained and lacks concentration. To the dog the possibly older track he is following cannot be as interesting as the fresh track of the hare which has just crawled away at his approach.

Most people will say that the dog is following a blood scent – but many hounds and tracker dogs follow unhurt beasts through all difficulties and the blood scent may be very weak. It is hard to believe that a wing-tipped pheasant leaves much blood scent behind him. Let a police dog sniff the scent on the possessions of a criminal and he will follow that scent through all distractions, but then, of course, he is specially trained for this particular task. Another suggestion is that this faculty is the result of a very old instinct. A dog who is following a trail, although he knows the quarry is far away, will ignore a new trail because his instinct tells him that if he continually changes and follows fresh game he will never come up with the quarry, but if he continues to follow the old trail he will wear his prey down. In the old days the wolves who followed a trail to the end may have done better than those who didn't, and it is therefore an example of the survival of the fittest.

A dog can no doubt distinguish between a shot pheasant with the scent of blood upon it and an unshot bird which has made itself scarce. A dog can also differentiate between one pheasant and another.

Training teaches the dog, through association which is built up on his inherited instinct to stick to a trail, that it is the shot bird his master wants while the unshot bird will not only take wing and fly away but his master will reprimand him if he chases. A shooting dog who hears the pellets hit the bird, watches it fall, hears the thump as it hits the ground, will rush out to the fall, ignoring all other distractions. Then, having acknowledged the fall, it will know the smell of that particular bird and will follow its trail, if it has run – he has learnt that there will be a dead or wounded bird at the end.

It's probably a combination of these factors which makes a dog decide to stick to one particular line. On the whole, we think it's the inherited instinct of the beast which is the principal factor which makes him decide that, once he is on a trail, he will follow it to its logical conclusion, but that blood scent certainly adds relish to the scent for gun dogs.

Trainers talk of 'a dog with a good nose'. It is not suggested that a greyhound, which runs on sight, and a bloodhound or American Coon Hound have the same scenting ability. It is suggested, however, that most labradors, being of the same breed, have about equal noses, as, in fact, they have equal vision (excluding pathological conditions). It's not the dog's actual nose that counts, but his powers of concentration. This can be seen in a young dog who, having sniffed a scent, will hunt wildly around and then appear to forget all about it, while an experienced dog, having caught the faintest scent, will hunt very close and work it out. An interesting example of this is when a tennis ball is hit on to very hard ground, bounces several large bounces and then rolls a good way into a ditch. The dog finds the first bounce, hunts very close and acknowledges succeeding bounces and finally tracks the ball into the ditch, finding it immediately. A dog who was thought to have a bad nose never seemed to do well on dummies, and in fact never 'eye-wiped' another dog on a dummy, but on the shooting field and in trials he demonstrated that he could smell after all. So again we come back to the question of owning a dog of the right temperament who does not over-run his nose and has sufficient brain power to concentrate on the job in hand. While a dog's memory is selective and he has an amazing memory for scents – once smelt, never forgotten – he has to learn to use his nose, and some dogs never do. It is the quality of the young dog, not his nose, we have to look for.

A strong odour can fatigue a dog's nose until he no longer smells it if it is continuous, but in the scenting we are discussing not only are the smells very faint but they are also intermittent, so fatigue does not often take place. However, if there is a very strong scent present a dog's nose will have to be fatigued until he cannot smell it before he will be able to smell the scent which we wish him to follow.

> In Koln a town of monks and bones,
> And pavements fanged with murderous stones
> And rags and hags and hideous wenches
> I counted two and seventy stenches . . .

If the poet Coleridge could differentiate seventy-two stenches, how many more could a dog differentiate!

A dog following a runner may be using ground scent, air scent or both. Now we all hope that our dog will acknowledge the fall, put his nose down and proceed along the track without check at a fair pace; but, of course, this seldom happens, especially with young dogs. If your dog is up-wind of the running bird he will have to use ground scent, as all the scent from the track and the bird is being blown away from him.

If the runner has run across-wind, the dog may elect to use air scent if it is good and runs parallel, though down-wind of the track and always at some distance from it, but the scent must be good.

If, however, he is down-wind of the bird, the air scent will have blown towards him and be dispersed more widely the further he is from the bird, inversely becoming fainter and fainter – there is a cone of scent present. Thus he has three methods of deciding which way the bird has run, how far away it is and in what direction. With the increasing intensity of the air scent as he nears the bird and the decreasing dispersal of the scent as he quests from side to side, he can get a fair impression of which way the bird has gone and how far away it is; he also has the ground scent getting stronger and stronger. Back-tracking is very important in trail hounds and they have to learn not to do it. We usually send our dogs to the fall, so there is only one direction in which they can go, but they do track back. Occasionally, practice on too many runners harms a young dog, making him excitable, even hard-mouthed, and training on runners should be left until a dog is fully trained. Training with tennis balls and some experience in the shooting field combined with the natural instinct of the dog should be enough. However, there is no doubt that the chief duty of a retriever is to find wounded game. Some dogs are particularly clueless in this respect, but at trials one often sees the beautiful behaviour of the Queen's dogs on runners. They, of course, get plenty of practice. The rules of field trials have been modified a little and the handler is not necessarily out of a trial for a first dog down failure on a runner provided that the dog has made a reasonable attempt to acknowledge the fall and hunt.

Practice on runners should be confined to fully trained dogs and also to mature dogs. The terms are not similar – a fully trained dog can still be very immature and puppyish. Having accepted this, there are several ways of making a track without leaving your own track:

(1) By using a long fishing line and always walking in circles down-wind of the track you wish to lay.
(2) By enlisting the help of a friend and tying the bird half-way between you and your friend.

Having said this, there is no objection initially to allowing the dog to get the right idea by dragging a freshly killed bird behind you so that the dog can follow both your track and the bird. There is a slight objection to using fur to make a track since this might encourage chasing. Again, there is no objection initially to using dummies to make a track, as long as the track is a short one – after all, we use dummies for all other kinds of training. There are, however, certain rules:

(1) The track must be laid so that the dog works up-wind to the bird on a good scenting day.
(2) The dog must be sent to a 'drop' which must be well marked out by rubbing the bird over a fairly large area.
(3) The drop must be marked by a pole so that you know exactly where the drop is.
(4) The track must not be too long until the dog is fully trained.
(5) The training should commence with warm, freshly killed game, and then can continue with cold game.
(6) The training must not be repeated too often.

Our dogs are poor performers on the whole as compared with a dog whose job is tracking; this is because we train a dog to search an area with a stationary dummy and we are always stopping him from following hare tracks, or hunting out of the area, or chasing. Having drilled him in these measures, we now expect him to work miracles on wounded game!

IV

A Discussion on Faults

'Shrieking and squeaking in fifty different sharps and flats.'

Yipping and Hard Mouth

Squeaking is an emotional response, as opposed to barking, which is an instinctive response. Here is the history of four squeakers. The first two were mother and daughter. The mother would only yip if she was swimming to collect a seen retrieve – this was frustration in that she could not swim fast enough. The daughter would only yip when a dog was working right in front of her – this was jealousy. Both achieved considerable success in field trials, one became a champion and the other just missed it; both were sent out of a trial for being noisy, but in both cases the tendency was kept to some degree under control by firmness, though never cured. They were both extremely garrulous in their old age.

The other two dogs were rather different. One, having run three trials successfully but at rather short intervals, started yipping in the fourth trial while still in the shooting brake and only lasted the first ten minutes of the trial. He had had the habit to a slight degree even as a small puppy when excited, and the cause of his yipping was nervous tension and excitement. He was temperamentally unsuited for trials and shooting. The fourth in the middle of a trial suddenly started yipping and yowling uncontrollably – this was pure hysteria.

A barking dog who, after all, is only giving his instinctive warning response can be cured by association. The quickest way is by using an electric collar which the Americans have produced with a built-in microphone tuned to a dog's bark so that every time the dog barks he gets a shock. Don't try it on your own neck or the dog may bark and set it off.

A squeaking dog cannot be cured: he has a basic emotional fault, often, as shown above, with a strong hereditary factor. It is said that yipping is infectious, as certainly hysteria is, and, as is well known, a dog reacts to the nervous tension of his master and can have trial nerves. If there is the slightest tendency to squeak, association with a squeaker will, by exciting the other dog, encourage squeaking and make him worse – but a non-squeaker will not be made to squeak by association with a squeaker. It is the emotional tension which is infectious. Whether hard mouth and yipping occur frequently in the same animal is debatable. Theoretically they should not, because hard mouth in non-acquired cases is an instinctive reaction which has been bred out of the breed over the course of many years, but which, like all instincts, crops up occasionally in future generations. Obviously all dogs were hard mouthed originally. We are, of course, aided because our dogs only occasionally collect live game and the dog knows that there is no point in killing a dead bird twice. Squeaking, however, is an emotional fault – in fact, a dog should instinctively be quiet while hunting unless he is hunting in a pack, and even pack animals do not hunt all the year round as a pack but only at certain seasons.

A few words can be said here about hard mouth. A young dog may through excitement tend to crush the game it is sent to collect, but this does not of necessity mean that the dog is hard mouthed. If care is taken not to allow it to get too excited, and to introduce it to game slowly and in quiet conditions, the incipient fault can probably be overcome. A dog should not be introduced to game at too early a stage in his career. It must also be admitted that at some time in their careers most dogs crush a bird. Having said this, it must also be explained that a really hard-mouthed dog must be discarded as there is no cure. Dogs have been seen to crush hares and are quite frequently seen really biting at birds as they bring them in. The borderline cases are more difficult to judge – when the judge or handler feels the ribs of the bird well up under the wings they should be round, and not flat or concave. However, some birds are very soft, and in doubtful cases the judge should err towards mercy and give the handler further retrieves. It is a different matter, however, if the ribs are not standing. It is interesting to note what little pressure is required to break the ribs of a bird. Ribs may even break while a judge is examining a bird for hard mouth – a bird which has not been crushed by the dog. The handler should himself always examine every bird his dog retrieves.

The owner of a good-going, hard-mouthed, headstrong yipper has only one hope –that he also has the digging instinct, which will at least save his master the trouble of digging a grave.

Clewing up

A dog has a definite personality and therefore his reactions to any set of circumstances are never certain. Some dogs are eager to learn, concentrate on their lessons and seem to need only one demonstration of an exercise for them to grasp it. Others refuse to concentrate, let their minds wander and sit contemplating the distant view. Some dogs are naturally thick and some dogs become bored very quickly with dummies. Some dogs are of a happy disposition, and others tend to sulk, but all dogs will clew up under certain circumstances.

If a dog is given too many retrieves and kept training too long, he will become thick, slow and disobedient. This is not the dog's fault and he should be taken home. If a dog is frustrated too many times by stopping him on seen retrieves or not letting him hunt freely, he will tend to clew up. A dog must be left to work things out for himself. The trainer must at times positively encourage him, even though the dog's performance is not all that brilliant, if he feels that his dog has been negatively trained to too great an extent.

A dog, if he is over-punished, will clew up and refuse to take any positive action – this is the confusion caused by pain and is a neurotic reaction. He will also become stupid and lose interest if he is given too difficult a job, and hence all training exercises should be simple. Finally, if a dog is sent out too far on a blind retrieve, he may lose confidence in himself and sit down and do nothing, or hunt in a desultory manner or become disobedient. The cure of most of these examples lies with the trainer, but in the last instance there are several courses of action from which to choose. The trainer can go out, chastise the dog and then, standing near him, get him to hunt and obey orders, very quickly directing him on to the dummy he is supposed to be retrieving. This is probably the best method for the average dog. Alternatively the trainer may call him in, praise him extravagantly as if he had done well, give him a simple retrieve or two to restore his confidence and a few direction signals to re-establish obedience, then take him home.

The following day the trainer must repeat the circumstances and so arrange things that the conditions are not quite so severe; until the dog is doing well again.

An interesting experiment

It was after a working test and three of us were standing together with our fully trained dogs. It was suggested that we tried to send our dogs out to a pond over 300 yards away and that dummies should be put out, as even a trained dog is better not sent out unless there is something to collect. So one of us walked out and put down three dummies on the edge of the pond. When he came back he suggested that he send out his dog first, knowing that he would have no difficulty – not only had the dog seen his master go out, but there was a double track for the dog to follow. It was a good-going dog. It went out at full gallop, collected a dummy, and came back as fast. We pointed out to him that this was no test. The next handler had the advantage of seeing the first dog go out straight; also there were two dummies to collect. The dog went out straight, stopping every 50 yards for directions, and finally sat down about 250 yards out and refused to move or take direction signals. He was at the limit of his confidence so the handler walked forward 50 yards and repeated the forward signal. The dog obeyed, went into the pond, from which his master recalled him, hunted on command and brought the dummy back. He praised him extravagantly, gave him one of his ham sandwiches (without mustard) and was obviously happy and pleased. The third dog went out reasonably well, but stuck at 250 yards, started hunting and being disobedient to signals. His master went out and chastised him and then made him pick the dummy. When he came back, he said, 'If I give an order, my dog must obey.' He was wrong in this particular case as the order was unreasonable at that distance and the dog was not disobeying through wilfulness but through lack of confidence and confusion.

V

Some General Aspects of Training

'Keep ye the law, be swift in all obedience.'

There is a saying that the only dog worth training is one that doesn't need it. Many people will disagree with this – but there are in the main two types of dogs.

There is, on the one hand, the fast, good-going dog. He is often difficult to train and in the wild would in all probability be the pack leader with the brain and drive to initiate the hunt. He would be the fastest dog, so he would lead the chase and organize the kill. He would be sufficiently dominant to hold his position and in the wild would be the fittest and have the pick of the food and the choice of the most attractive bitches; he would not only have the pick of the pack for his mate but would have the strength to hold her against the rest. In this way Nature ensures that only the best survive to breed. If this is the pack leader in the wild, surely it follows that if this type of dog is properly trained – and emphasis must be laid on the word 'properly' – he is exactly the kind of dog required by a field-trial enthusiast. Some of these dogs are so dominant and wilful that they will only grasp the object of an exercise after countless repetitions, and then it takes ages to sink in. The trainer can spend many hours on a hard, fast, good-going dog and may completely fail in his endeavours, the result being an animal who cannot be trusted, is even harder and who goes further in the wrong direction. He may and does win trials under an experienced trainer, but is of little use to the ordinary shooting man as he will take advantage of him before he has got his gun cleaned at the end of the first day of the season. A fast, good-going dog need not necessarily be brash and headstrong, but often is.

On the other hand, there is the biddable little dog. Some dogs have only to be shown an exercise and they appear to grasp it straight away – you can almost see them thinking. Sensitivity, however, must not be confused with timidity. A

Which? – on being sold a pup!

sensitive, biddable little dog can be very courageous. In this
type of dog confidence can be built up gradually. Nobody,
however, wants a lethargic animal or a problem dog, however
biddable the latter may be. Any dog, however biddable, will
go wild and get out of hand if not kept under control. Moreover if taken out shooting by a man who treats him as a gun,
takes him out only on shooting days and ignores him for the
remainder of the time, the quiet, biddable little beast will
soon become as wild and wilful as the rest.

In finding a youngster the trainer therefore has two choices.
But whatever type he chooses, not only should he acquire the
beast young enough – at the very latest six months old – but
having purchased it, he should also give the dog time to
mature. A good many of us tend to forget how long it takes a
dog to gain maturity of mind and that experience which only
time can teach. A dog does not reach full maturity until he is
about four years old. The average amateur trainer should aim
for a biddable puppy which comes from biddable stock and has
style.

Training begins at a very early age and good habit patterns
can be built up without disturbing the puppy's natural joy in
existence – the puppy's natural instinct is to follow, to hunt,
to carry things, and these should be built on gradually.
Later on one can pick out the honest dogs from the dishonest
ones. At a field trial a trainer was running two dogs. She came
out of the line and said that with one of them, if a bird had
been shot, she had to look directly at him, never taking her
eyes off him, or he would run in. This was a dishonest dog.
The other one in similar circumstances she dare not look at
directly, but watched him out of the corner of her eye,
because if she looked at him directly he would wish to go out
and retrieve. However, as long as she did not look directly he
was steady. This was an honest dog. While training the
second dog she decided to put some pressure on him. After
the punishment he crawled away on his belly into a corner,

put his head between his paws and shut his eyes on the principle that, if he couldn't see his mistress, his mistress couldn't see him. This was the end of her attempts to put pressure on this particular animal.

An honest dog, when a bird is shot, will look up at his trainer; if the trainer shakes his head and formulates the word 'no' with his lips, as likely as not he will accept this, lie down and start chewing grass.

The Dog and his Master

A dog can neither respect his master nor give loyalty. A dog can recognize authority in the voice of a stranger who has not trained him. A dog can love his master's smell if he is present, but soon after he has gone he no longer thinks about it. And he can be obedient to his master's commands. His master, however, is capable of respect – he can respect the hen pheasant on her nest in the hedgerow even though he is going to shoot her later, or the bullock in the field, which he is going to eat; and he must respect his dog, allowing him his comforts and privileges, but he must exact a habit of obedience from him. As soon as his dog leaves the kennel he must come immediately to heel without being told; he should wait till he is told to get into or out of the car. In the shooting field he must ignore other dogs and not wander from his master's side; if he is told to stay, his master must be able to walk away and talk to a friend, and he must not move, even though other dogs are milling around. Such obedience, we hope, is willing. A dog does not blame or hate the master who punishes him, but he can associate the presence of the master with fear.

In Nature there are no punishments, only consequences. A dog can learn obedience through punishment, but as fear and pain paralyse and confuse, this is an unthinking and unwilling obedience. To obtain a willing obedience it is necessary to take

43

into account the rest of the dog's life. If a dog is allowed out of kennels only to work or to take so-called exercise – which is really a chance to allow him to defecate – he gets a kennel mind. He will become bored and frustrated, and possibly neurotic. It has been said that a dog in kennels does not acquire bad habits, but neither does he build up all the associations necessary for him to lead a happy and contented life. It is widely thought by the public that mongrels are more intelligent than pure-bred dogs – if this is true it is because a mongrel is seldom kennelled but wanders about and picks up many associations. However, there are many highly intelligent true-bred dogs. A dog kept continuously on a chain soon grows neurotic and very bad tempered. The most stupid dogs are those which have been kept rigidly in kennels during the first twelve months of their lives. Play is necessary to dogs of all ages – even old dogs will play with young ones if they like each other – and by playing is not meant the order 'go and play' when all the dogs rush off and run around. This is good but is really a demonstration of the pack instinct. But a couple of dogs, if allowed out in a large run, will play for hours together. Dogs should be allowed and encouraged to play with the trainer's wife and children. A trainer should play with his dog in a somewhat more restrained manner and then re-establish instant and immediate obedience if the dog becomes too excited. It is nice to see a couple of dogs playing together, rolling each other over, snarling and ambushing each other. No dog will prosper if he is under discipline all the time, nor if he is in kennels; it is in this respect that the trainer who has only a few dogs and can allow them in the house with the children, letting them play together, has the advantage over the trainer who has many dogs.

The difficulty with training, and especially with direction signals with biddable dogs, is that it curbs the natural abilities of the dog who becomes too dependent. This is why the stultifying effects of kennels have been explained together with the necessity of allowing the dog adequate freedom when he is not under control and the great importance of play. On the other hand, harsh treatment also curbs his natural ability. We all fully understand the necessity of having a free-running dog. The maxim that should be engraved on every trainer's heart is 'Let the dog work it out for himself', or, as has been said elsewhere, 'Trust your dog.'

If we read training books of sixty or seventy years ago, before field trials had really commenced, we learn that directing a dog to the fall was considered unnecessary, but that great emphasis was laid on the hunting ability of the dog and how to train him to this end and also to the retrieving of runners. If we are to get the best out of our dogs, we must always remember that, although an experienced trainer with a well-trained dog can win trials, the shooting man's ideal is a dog which will give him no worries while he is shooting, but which, having been sent out after a shot bird, will persevere and find that bird with no help from his master. It is, however, our opinion that any good shooting dog should be able to acquit itself well in a novice field trial.

Some time ago, a dog who had been trained too much in an open field, and instructed always to get over hedges and ditches, had lost the instinct to hunt ditches and runnels. It was, therefore, necessary to invent a new word of command – 'seek in'. This was, of course, accompanied by the necessary signal to hunt. From then on, if the dog had been sent over the ditch or hedge his next retrieve would be a dummy in the hedge bottom with the command 'seek in'. The fault was, of course, easy to correct as a natural instinct (to hunt cover) was being encouraged, but it is an example of how errors can creep in, in training.

When a dog is fully trained and has reached some maturity, the trainer usually finds that, although the training period may have been a hard struggle, now the dog is eager to train and will pick up lessons quickly. A dog will always have diffi-

Often a duck gets tucked in under a bank

culty in finding a bird which has lodged off the ground on a
bush or in the branch of a tree. Retrieves should be arranged
with the bird or dummy in this position and, if the dog
cannot find, he should be shown where the bird is. After a
few retrieves, if he cannot find on the ground he will lift his
head and search at a higher level.

Often a duck gets tucked in under the bank of a river and
the dog may swim past it or pass it on the bank without
scenting it. The trainer must learn to hold his dog and by
pointing downwards persuade the dog to drop his head so
that he can scent the duck. A few retrieves of this nature and
the dog will realize what is required and it may stand the
trainer in good stead at a later date.

During this period in a dog's life, he should be trained to
be steady while sitting about 5 to 10 yards away from his

master. This is probably best practised when picking up at drives in the hope that a bird or two will fall near him.

A dog at this time of his training should be allowed to pick a wounded hare, to see that he can cope with it. It should first be seen that the hare is not likely to run, as even at this stage chasing hares must be prevented. The rule for hares is as follows: during the first season let your dog pick a couple of hares to see that he can carry them; in the second season expose your dog to as many hares as possible to ensure his steadiness; and in the third season let him pick a wounded hare. If a wounded duck is diving on a pond – where, with a half-trained dog, the retrieve should be refused – now, with your fully trained animal, the retrieve should be welcomed.

Steady at heel

VI

Some Special Methods of Training

' 'E don't obey no orders unless they is 'is own.'

Training by Food

Training by food is almost a dirty phrase in the field trial world, yet all circus people use food to train their animals to perform tricks. We also use food on occasions for, if it is carefully used, food can be of great service. All puppies should be trained to sit while their food is being prepared – this is only normal discipline – and they can be made to lift their heads up by holding the bowl above their heads and giving them a mouthful to eat. They are taught not to snatch and to take the food from your hand gently – if they are certain that the food is going to be given them and the hand that gives it is not going to be pulled back at the last moment. A very young puppy can be trained to hunt and to use his nose by hiding pieces of food and letting him try to find them. This is good training if not carried to excess, but should be abandoned when he learns to carry dummies. Food is used to get him accustomed to gunfire and other loud noises, by subjecting him to them when he is eating, or feeding him in the car if he is frightened of travelling by car. These are the

48

normal uses for food which most of us employ. It has been noticed, however, that even though you may have fired shots while the puppy is feeding, this does not necessarily make him accept gunfire while training him at a later date, and he may still dislike gunfire until trained to appreciate it.

A dog which is fully fed is lethargic and wishes to sleep. In Nature, following a large meal an animal will sleep for hours until hunger wakes him again. A hungry dog on the contrary is alert, active and keen on hunting – thus following his natural instincts. It is, therefore, well worth arranging your training sessions when a dog is really hungry, even delaying his meal well past his normal feeding time. This would especially apply if you have a lethargic dog or some training difficulty: a hungry dog learns quickly. Giving a piece of food as a reward or, as is better said, as a method of impressing the association which we have been trying to teach on to the dog's memory, is slightly more difficult and has to be handled with care; certainly a dog would rather receive a mouthful of food than have his chest scratched and receive some words of praise. But, for example, if you are trying to teach your dog to come back quickly and willingly to you, he must come back, sit, raise his head, and deliver the dummy before you give him the food, and then must take it gently from your hand. If he does badly he does not get the food. At the end of the training session he finishes up his meal. This method of reinforcing a lesson must not be used to excess and is most useful if there is some training difficulty – and it is certain that any method which will make a dog obey an order willingly, wagging his tail and happy, is superior to getting obedience through fear of the consequences and punishment. It should be emphasized that the whole purpose of praise or of giving a mouthful of food, or scratching a dog's chest, is to reinforce the association you are teaching him; it should never be omitted in training and should be continued throughout a dog's life – even when he is mature. Praise never hurt anybody.

Under the influence of hunger the wild animal shows a very great degree of perseverance. This ability of an animal to persevere appears to be rather lacking in our dogs today. After a relatively short hunt they lose interest, hunt wildly, or 'clew up'. If it is so arranged that your dog associates the finding of the dummy with getting his food and appeasing his hunger, then we may be able to improve his hunting qualities.

A dog who is frightened of strangers can be tempted by food to accept them if he is hungry. Food is therefore a stronger method of impressing a lesson on a dog's mind than the usual method of praise – but should not be used as a routine, only as an exception if some difficulty is experienced. Different dogs' reaction to food varies considerably. Some are excessively greedy; with others the trainer finds great difficulty in making the dog take an interest in food. The object of the exercise is to make the dog wish to obey the trainer happily while wagging his tail. If this can be accomplished by a judicious association of food with the trainer, all is well and it helps with the training. Food can also be used to train a dog to face cover, and nettles – a method of using food described later on in the book.

It would be nice if sex could be used in training – and in one way it can. A bitch just before her heat seems to run a little above her form. Unfortunately, sex conquers all – it seems too great an urge to be used constructively. A pigeon fancier was describing how, in this permissive society, he uses sex: when a pair of pigeons is billing and cooing in complete domestic bliss, he puts a strange cock bird in the next cage and, having made the husband jealous, dispatches him to France from where he returns with utmost speed, beating his previous record – or, alternatively, when the hen is nicely settled in her new home, he sends her away, and instead of indulging herself in light dalliance in a foreign field, she also comes swiftly home.

The Use of Electricity in Training

This method of training does not seem to have become very popular in England, but we saw it demonstrated in America where it appears to be used quite extensively. The apparatus is expensive and possibly appeals particularly to Americans, who are more gadget-minded than we are. There are several varieties of apparatus.

The simplest method is the *electric stick* – if a dog, for example, goes forward when at heel, the trainer says 'back', and if he does not obey, touches him with the stick and gives him a shock. The dog, however, would soon become frightened of any stick and start cringing whenever he saw a man carrying one – it is, of course, similar to the electric goad used in the cattle markets.

The *electric lead* is for training to walk on a lead; instead of using a choke collar and jerking the dog back as we do, the trainer says 'heel' and, if he does not obey, gives him a shock through the lead. It can, of course, also be used with a check cord. Our methods are simpler and effective, and probably these two gadgets are really intended for the lay public.

Electricity has also been used to cure dogs of eating their own faeces in the same manner that we use electric fencing – if the dog touches the faeces he gets a shock.

The *electric collar* with built-in microphone reacting to a dog's bark is used to stop dogs from barking. Here it is effective – so much so that an American complained that his dog never barked now, whoever came to the door. Finally, there is the electric collar with a wireless transmitter.

A dog is more sensitive to electric shocks than we are, and the current is so arranged that the dog jerks his head around when the shock is administered. If the shock is too strong it can even knock him down. The dog must always wear the collar, or dummy weighted similarly, otherwise he will learn to associate the collar with the shocks. The collar must not be used when the dog is near any electrical machine giving out impulses, such as an electric mower. The usual rules of training are observed, an order is given: the dog knows what the order is about, he defies the order and therefore gets punished by the shock. Whether the dog associates the trainer with the punishment is a point of importance. When a dog is punished, it is desirable for him to associate the trainer with the disobedience; a dog should never be punished sufficiently severely to make him either confused by fear or unwilling to come back happily to the trainer to be caressed.

The claim is made that using the electric trainer considerably shortens the time necessary to train a dog, and in those brash dogs who require a considerable amount of negative training, this is true, but with a biddable dog all that is required is your voice and an occasional shake. On occasion, however, an electric collar could be invaluable. It must be very satisfying, when your dog is out and puts up a hare or a rabbit and starts a glorious chase, to press that button, or to use it to chastise a dog who has to be cured of chicken chasing. It would be a great boon to a professional trainer who has to train for other people dogs which have already developed faults, and who has also to train many dogs in a short time. However, it should only be used when in difficulties.

The Uses of a Check Cord

A check cord is used not only to control a dog but also to teach the dog that he is under control at a distance. Unfortunately, the dog eventually learns that when the cord is removed the power of control ceases, and so he tends to get disobedient again. This can to some extent be avoided by shortening the cord and letting the dog drag the shortened cord free after training by the long cord has been completed but before removing it altogether. For a time, he will still associate the shortened cord with the long one and conform. Normally check-cord training is used only for short periods and as little as possible. However, with one dog who would not approach the handler, the check cord was attached as soon as the dog left the car and was not removed until the dog returned to the car at the end of training; this was persisted with every day for weeks until the habit was completely broken. The shortened cord is also useful in that it can be stamped on if the dog happens to be disobedient when he is near you. The cord should be as light and inconspicuous as possible. A fishing line is an ideal check cord, and if a reel is used as well it prevents many tangles. It is not necessary to use a check cord if training is commenced from a small puppy; training may be made so gradual that one stage is mastered before the next is begun – one of the advantages which emphasizes the importance of early training – but it is understood that with a dog bought at a year old or over, a check cord is not only convenient but even essential, and will shorten the time taken in training quite considerably.

A check cord is used in the following manner. The cord having been tied round the dog's neck – since if you attach it to a choke chain the cord falls off – the dog is put up and the trainer walks away. If the dog starts to move, a flick on the cord and the command 'up' is given. If the trainer wishes the dog to come to him, he signals the dog in. If the dog is disobedient, he walks down the cord to the dog, pats and reassures him, then walks a little way off again and repeats the command. He never drags the dog in by the cord. After these exercises have been mastered, the trainer throws a dummy a little way away and sends the dog again. If the dog tries to run away with the dummy, a hard jerk on the cord and the word 'no', then the dog is signalled in. If this fails again the trainer walks down the cord and reassures the dog.

The two main rules of check-cord training are: never drag the dog by the cord and always give a command before you jerk the cord so that disobedience to the command is associated with a jerk. If on retrieving a dog tries to rush past the trainer, the trainer stamps on the cord as the dog passes him so that he is brought up with a jerk. Again the dog is patted in, and praised for coming in.

The cord can be used for training to the stop whistle, especially for overcoming that annoying habit some dogs acquire of running on a yard or two before obeying it. A dog must obey the stop whistle immediately.

From time to time when cord training has been mastered these exercises are practised with a shortened cord lying free, and then without a cord, but at the least sign of disobedience the cord is attached again.

Forced Training

Dogs can often be very stubborn, which is a different problem from not understanding what is required of them. So it is necessary at times to 'force' them to do what the trainer wants. When you are training a puppy to heel on a lead and you jerk him back every time he runs ahead of you, you are using force methods.

If a dog drops his head on delivery and you pull his head up by the ears, you are forcing him to raise his head. And on a check cord, if a dog refuses to come to you and you pull him in by the check cord, and then when he is dragged to your feet you praise him, you are still using force methods.

The most typical example of this method is when a dog refuses to pick a dummy or spits it out every time it is just in his mouth; to cure this you might then twist his ear or tread on his toe, force the dummy into his mouth and every time he tries to spit it out increase the pain and discomfort; but,

A hard jerk on the check cord

as long as he holds it in his mouth, talk and gentle him. Force methods have to be used at times, and are so used on difficult and awkward dogs, but, as emphasized previously, all pain confuses. All training methods, moreover, should be positive and not negative. If you take the two examples given above, the jerk on the lead to force a puppy to heel is positive, but dragging him in by the check cord is negative.

Keeping a puppy stationary by a check cord while you walk up to him is, of course, a different matter. The pulling of a dog's head up by the ears or the twisting of his ears when he spits out a dummy are all negative. The reaction of the dog on these occasions is to pull away from the check cord, or to drop his head even lower when you lift his head by his ears. It is really as simple as teaching a dog to sit: push his behind down and he will rear it up; lift his chin up and his behind will go down and he will sit. It requires as much patience to train a dog by force methods as by any other – in fact, probably more. However, as some intractable dogs do not respond to persuasion, these methods must be used. In terms of the mind, you are using pain as the association and not as the reinforcement.

In training dogs it must always be remembered that their

instinctive urges may be repressed or modified, but are always lying dormant and come to the surface at the most awkward times. A dog can be trained not to run in or chase. However, if conditions get hot he may forget his normal training, his instinctive urge being too strong, but if he has been trained by the electric collar – which, after all, is a force method, used in this case positively as the shock will stop him in mid-stride – he is unlikely to repeat the misdemeanour.

Portrait of F. Haworth

Portrait of J. A. Kersley

VII

A Dialogue on Difficulties

'It seems to be one of those simple cases which
is so extremely difficult.'

Heeling

1. The dog who is bad at heel, lags behind or jumps forward

PROBLEM: A 2-year-old dog who persists in heeling badly
sometimes drops behind, dodges from side to side, and if he
gets excited goes a yard or two in front of the handler – he
does not run in.

J.K.: Heeling is the natural instinct of a pack animal to follow a leader or another member of the pack, and training
for heeling is to modify and discipline this instinct so that
the dog takes up one position and stays there ignoring all
distractions, such as scents and tracks, until he is sent out.
F.H.: I think that if a dog has been trained properly he
should be a reasonable heeler – after all, he is close to you,
easily reprimanded, and if you can't keep him under control
at this distance, what chance have you got when he is out?
J.K.: Training for heeling should start immediately a dog
leaves the kennels; he is brought under control and should
be kept strictly at heel or sitting quietly by your side, until

he is sent out or allowed to go and play – it is an extension of the habit of obedience. Unfortunately, the average shooting man cares nothing for heeling. He allows his dog to wander all over the place and make a nuisance of itself between drives, and then expects his dog to be steady at other times. Training your dog to ignore scents when at heel will help very considerably to keep him steady and ignore the scent of game, unless it is wounded or dead game, when out working.

F.H.: One reason for jumping from side to side at heel is ill training. The trainer has smacked the dog on the nose for going in front on his left side and eventually the dog tries the same thing on the opposite side, to be met by the same treatment – it then acquires the habit of slipping from side to side. I have known such a dog to even trip up the handler.

J.K.: The dog who lags behind, usually has scented something that interests him – he is hunting at heel. A dog that heels well should have his head up, not sniffing the ground; he should know that all he has to do is concentrate on his master and mark game, and until he is sent out he should ignore everything else. A dog who goes forward is an over-excited dog. The only movement which is allowed him is to move so that he can see the mark.

F.H.: Poor heeling should never occur if adequate practice with firm discipline has been instituted from early days, and if the dog has never been allowed to wander round, whether he is among other dogs or guns or with you alone. Bad heeling indicates a somewhat excitable dog with poor training by the handler. To cure bad heeling, walk the dog continually on the lead and choke chain, giving a very sharp and pointed jerk each time he strays from a position right at heel. This practice should continue day after day until the bad habit he has acquired has either been forgotten by the dog or overcome by the trainer. It's quite easy to

Dogs should be steady if left

train a dog to heel by placing the choke chain round the dog's neck with the dog on the left side, and holding the lead firmly in the right hand; the lead is then stretched across the front of the thigh. With each stride taken, the left leg moves forward pulling the dog level with you. If this exercise is done regularly the dog learns to keep level with you, and he finds it impossible not to do so. Alternatively, the lead can be stretched across the back of your thighs, forcing the dog back.

2. *The dog who refuses to keep in the line*

PROBLEM: At a field trial or a formal shoot the dog lags 20 yards behind the handler and refuses to walk at heel when called up.

60

F.H.: One type of this kind of dog is 'root shy'. He is perfectly good at heel in stubble or on grassland, but not in
roots where he is frightened of the noise and density of it.
The other type always lags 20 yards behind when there is
a line-out on plain fields or stubble as he is frightened of
the strange guns, beaters, and more particularly of the sticks
the beaters wave.

J.K.: No dog should ever be chastised with a stick, otherwise
whenever he sees a stick waved he associates it with punishment. He might even become gun-shy if he thinks the gun
is a stick. A short length of rubber or leather strap is the
correct instrument for punishing a dog. This type of dog
has been left too much in kennels and has not associated
sufficiently with strange human beings and noise.

F.H.: He has either been beaten and frightened or has not
been humanized.

J.K.: I have twice lost my dog when he should have been at
my heel at trials. In the first instance, we were in line on
plain fields – I looked down and saw my dog was heeling
on the judge! I tried to attract his attention, but no, that
dog loved that judge. A pheasant got up, the dog froze,
the judge looked down at the dog and then beckoned me
towards him and said, 'I am the judge, you know. Don't
you think it is time you handled your own dog!'

The other time was in very thick kale. There was my
black dog and a yellow labrador in the line. I had heard the
rustle of a dog at my heels, and as we came out of the
kale, I looked down and to my consternation saw a yellow
labrador at my heel. I looked wildly round and there, 30
yards away, was my black labrador sitting at the heel of
the other handler. I thought, the judge will never notice
as long as he has a black and a yellow in the line, so I
walked over and engaged him in conversation. The other
handler had the same idea. When we parted, we each had
the right dog at our heels!

Even kneel down to make oneself less awe-inspiring

F.H.: We haven't cured our bad heeler yet and I think we are both agreed that all that is required is patience and kindness. Also, take the dog about with you until he is completely used to human beings, noise and other dogs. Encourage him to walk at heel by praise, wave a stick or a gun about but, of course, never touch him with it. Try in every way to restore his confidence. There should be no real difficulty. And, of course, every dog should have plenty of training and experience in crops.

Delivery

3. The dog who won't deliver to hand

PROBLEM: A dog was bought at 12 months old. It refused to approach the handler to deliver the dummy. After the fault was apparently cured it recurred again when the dog was 20 months old. It is thought that the dog may have been harshly treated as a puppy.

F.H.: Two thoughts occur to my mind – firstly, that you should never buy a dog at 12 months old unless you know 'the stable' from which it has come, and secondly, a dog has a very long memory of events that occur in puppyhood. It is very difficult to eradicate a fault acquired in early training.

J.K.: I agree. I suppose that, when you first got the dog, after getting to know it you tried patting it in and praising it without a dummy, and then with a dummy. Probably you ran away from it when it was coming to deliver and even knelt down to make yourself less awe-inspiring on delivery – in fact, you used the usual training tricks.

F.H.: These methods seemed to succeed, after about a month's persistent training. So I continued with its normal training, then the fault recurred, so I started to use a light check cord.

J.K.: I don't use check cords, but I think this was one of the times when a check cord was necessary. You used it in the ordinary way, controlling the dog with it and thus stopping him getting away. You hoped he would come up to you when he realized he was under control, but you never dragged the dog towards you.

F.H.: The dog persisted in the fault, so I started training in a fairly narrow passage with one end blocked. You sit the dog beside you and throw the dummy, as you have been doing in a normal training session. The dog will run out and pick it up but he will be unable to go in any direction except towards you, and provided the passage is sufficiently narrow, he will be unable to pass you. So if he returns, sit him down, take the retrieve from him and give him lots of praise. If he picks the dummy and refuses to return, walk out after him trying not to frighten him, and encourage him to walk back at heel with the dummy in his mouth. When you reach the spot from which you threw the dummy, stop and take the dummy from the dog. This, done repeatedly, will cure the fault in that particular place. When you take the dog out into the field there's every chance that the fault will recur.

63

J.K.: The dog we're talking about was suspected of having had a harsh puppyhood. Was he acting in this manner because he was really a disobedient dog or because he was still nervous from his puppyhood experience?

F.H.: The dog, by this time, had had plenty of chances to overcome any puppyhood disabilities, so I started to put the pressure on. I used a choke chain and jerked him after I had spoken his name and then, when he came up, I gave him a pat.

J.K.: What happens if he starts dropping the dummy?

F.H.: I then replace it and make him hold it.

J.K.: There comes a time when there is a clash between you and your dog and you have to win. The more experienced you are in training and the more trouble you take, the less often these clashes recur.

4. *The dog who won't lift his head to deliver*

PROBLEM: A dog which on delivery, although maintaining his hold of the dummy, drops his head to the ground, thus making it difficult to take the game from him, and also looks exceedingly sloppy.

F.H.: Here, again, I think there has been bad training as a puppy. If you train a puppy to sit while preparing his meals – I hold a bowl over his head before giving it to him – he will learn to keep his head up. In any case, the normal training of a small puppy to retrieve and deliver should have prevented, in this case, a very ingrained fault from developing.

J.K.: Most dogs have minor degrees of this fault. One dog I know would always drop his head if you tried to take the dummy from him, but if you patted the top of his head with the left hand, he would raise his head for the pat and you could take the dummy out of his mouth with the right hand.

A Dialogue on Difficulties

F.H.: I think that both in tests and trials we are getting slack in our standards of delivery. Few dogs really deliver stylishly these days and you will see the handler taking large steps forward to grab the bird out of the dog's mouth before he drops it. This cannot be necessary if you trust your dog.

J.K.: What about the use of food to solve the problem? I must make one point, however. A dog must be trained to food in puppyhood before he can be trained by food in later life: that is to say, he must sit while his food is being prepared, and if hand-fed must only take it gently when told to do so.

F.H.: I am most definitely against the use of food. The result of doing this is that the dog most certainly will lift his head, but in order to get the food he will probably spit out the dummy; if this method is continued, he will rush back with his retrieve and, on approaching you, spit it out in order to get the titbit you are holding in your hand. I think you are thus likely to cause more faults than the one you are trying to cure.

J.K.: An attempt was made in this particular case to make the dog lift his head by pulling and twisting his ears so that he lifted his head to stop the discomfort. The dog instinctively tried to pull away from the pressure, and although this was persisted in for a considerable time, it was a total failure.

F.H.: The dog was finally cured by the trainer holding a fork in his hand and pressing it up under the dog's chin. The dog automatically lifted his head to get rid of the discomfort. After a time he would lift his head immediately the trainer put his hand under his chin and soon was delivering with style.

J.K.: This is the force method of training used positively – if pain is used to achieve results it must be used constructively.

5. The dog who refuses to approach the handler with a dummy

PROBLEM: A young dog, 9 months old, who circles the handler but refuses to come in and deliver.

J.K.: This is a persistence of the babyhood habit of wanting to play, but shows lack of training in puppyhood. It would be necessary to start from the very beginning to wait for the dog to come up to you or walk away and see if the dog will follow.

F.H.: The dog is fearful that you will take the dummy from him, so let him sit at your feet, holding the dummy until he looks like dropping it; and for the same reasons when he does come up to you with the dummy, praise him and caress him, but don't take the dummy from him until you think he is willing to give it up.

J.K.: I think also that basic discipline has not been taught the dog – he has not been taught to 'hup' on command – therefore 'hupping' exercises and exercises to sit, to stay there, to come in, are necessary.

F.H.: If, after these measures have been tried and there is still difficulty, he should be trained in the narrow passage, as we have described previously.

6. The dog who has an untidy delivery

PROBLEM: Untidy delivery takes many forms and occurs at all ages: (a) the dog may hold on to the bird and be loath to give it up; (b) the dog may go to your side instead of coming up to your knees in front; (c) the dog may stop a yard or so away from you instead of coming right up to you; or (d) the dog may tend to run past you.

F.H.: A dog holds on to a bird through possessiveness and one of the reasons for this is that you may be taking the bird away from him too quickly and without praising him before and after delivery of the bird. He can be made to disgorge by pressing his lip against his teeth at the angle of his mouth with your right thumb and then passing your thumb down to the back of his throat. Alternatively, you can squeeze his upper lips against his teeth with your hand over his muzzle – in any case, if you do this frequently enough he will dislike the discomfort and learn to deliver, preferably when you say 'dead'.

J.K.: A dog who delivers to your side is easily cured by taking his neck on each side with your hands, as if you were going to shake him, lift him half off the ground and swing him round and put him down in the correct position in front of you. I have noticed, however, that a dog who delivers perfectly on most occasions will suddenly for no very apparent reason deliver to the side. Perhaps it is the trainer who is at fault, who has not received his delivery in the immaculate fashion in which he expects his dog to behave.

F.H.: The dog who stops a yard away from you and does not come right up to your knees – there again, the handler may be at fault in that he has taken a step forward in order to take delivery. It also may possibly show some unwillingness on the part of the dog to give up the bird. If the handler steps back instead of standing still when taking the bird off the dog, the fault will soon be cured.

J.K.: The dog who tends to run past you – this is often caused because the dog has got up too much pace by the time he reaches you. Therefore, shorter retrieves should be given until the delivery is better. The retrieves should be arranged so that there is a hedge or gate at your back to make it difficult for the dog; if the fault persists the check cord is used and it is stamped on as the dog passes to bring him up with a jerk. Passage training as a puppy should have helped to obviate the fault. I find that most dogs do it for a time, but it is seldom persisted in.

Temperament

7. *The dog who is too brash (wilful)*

PROBLEM: An 18-months-old dog, who has been well trained, is good and obedient on the training field, but becomes disobedient when run in strange surroundings or at a working test.

J.K.: All these dogs are fast, good-going dogs, but I think they divide themselves into two types: the honest dog and the dishonest dog. The honest dog at heart wishes to please his master and disobeys from youthful exuberance and over-excitement in strange places. He is not at heart a hard dog. The dishonest dog only wishes to please himself and is always ready to defy his master. He is the really hard dog. The honest dog will look at you for instructions; the dishonest dog will not, unless he is forced to do so. It is difficult sometimes to distinguish between the two types, but I think the trainer who is with the dogs a lot can do so.

F.H.: It is important to differentiate between the two because the treatment is different. With the honest dog prolonged training is essential, first by yourself and then with as many people and dogs as possible and on as many different types of ground – a different one each day, always taking the dog back to the training ground if he misbehaves. Later take him on working tests, but be very careful not to take him on too many trials in succession – the dog has to be given time to mature. If the dog can be held, some of the most brilliant dogs can be found amongst this type. These dogs may benefit from being over-trained and then easing off.

J.K.: These dogs have to have firm discipline and must not be allowed to get away with things, but they also need a lot of praise if they do right. I think that they should be taken around with you a lot. You have to establish your authority as pack leader. I agree they take a long time to mature.

F.H.: The dishonest dog will never accept the trainer as his master and there is nothing that can be done except to administer hard discipline – to achieve any result at all the trainer would have to break the dog's spirit and then try and build from there: in fact, the old-fashioned method of 'breaking a dog'. These dogs are not worth training and are untrainable according to present-day ideas. They should be got rid of.

J.K.: I had a dog like this which I had trained for well over a year before deciding to get rid of him. During the fortnight before he left the kennels I took him out shooting but did not endeavour to keep him under the firm discipline I had previously maintained. During this short period he reverted to type and committed every crime in the dog calendar. These dogs are untrainable.

8. The dog who won't go into kennels

PROBLEM: A young dog 10-months-old, who has been brought up by a keeper, has been bought with a view to training for the gun and field trials – he dashes off and can't be approached whenever he is told to 'kennel up'.

F.H. and J.K. (in unison): We can't stand a dog that won't go into kennels.

J.K.: I can tell you some more about this particular dog. He had style and hunted beautifully, he could leap and showed courage, but he would dash off if he was approached and was extremely nervous and sensitive; in fact, completely unmanageable. One could not even think of training him until he was civilized.

F.H.: It was to some extent his upbringing in kennels. He

had never been humanized, and this combined with a strong hereditary factor – his parents were brilliant but one of them was very highly strung.

J.K.: I seem always to come back to the importance of very early training. I am beginning to think I am stressing it too much, but there are too many dogs who are neglected in their puppyhood.

F.H.: The cure for this dog was to take him into the house. He was, in fact, given away as a pet; there were children in the house and they gradually brought him round. In fact, children are the only people who can get through to such a dog as we have described. In this particular case the children were successful in that, although the dog was never trained for trials, which was a pity as he had great potential, he became a good and useful shooting dog of whom his master was proud, and I hope lived happily ever after.

J.K.: Let's talk about this problem in general. There are possibly two other kinds of dog who won't go into kennels. One rolls on his back and is submissive but reluctant to go in – on the whole a biddable dog. What would you do about that?

F.H.: Take him up by the scruff of his neck and throw him in.

J.K.: Then there is the rather brash youngster who tries to defy you – he is not a nervous dog.

F.H.: This is a symptom of a fault – brashness. You have to build up a habit of obedience and this is very basic. Either the dog is at play or under control. When he comes out of kennels he should go immediately to heel, and on return he should heel until the kennel door is opened and then go in on command. It is, after all, this instilling of general obedience that we as trainers have to work on.

J.K.: In the short term, I would give him a good shake, or one across the backside and order him in. In the long term I would tighten up my general handling of the dog.

9. The dog who is too highly strung or nervous

PROBLEM: A 12-months-old dog who shows all the signs of nervousness – is he worth training?

J.K.: I think it is worth while defining what is meant by a nervous dog. A nervous dog tends to run away home if he is spoken to or frightened; it trembles at the slightest touch and flinches. This must be distinguished from a dog who rolls on his back and is submissive – it hates noises, is frightened of thunder and is gun-nervous. A nervous dog is very suspicious of strangers and becomes too dependent on his master. He is difficult to train because if another dog is reprimanded, he takes the reprimand on to himself. A nervous dog may possibly snap or bite.

F.H.: He is easily made neurotic and then he refuses to do anything and just sits. I consider a nervous dog may be highly intelligent, but he is not necessarily a biddable dog – he may be when you are on your own without other people or other distractions, but when he is with other people he will urinate from nerves, crouch down and become useless.

J.K.: However intelligent he is, his fears confuse and paralyse his mind. I think the trainer has first to decide whether he has the qualities to make a good dog. If these qualities are present, if he has good hunting style, is fast, jumps boldly when there are no distractions, I think he is well worth training, and with patience you will overcome his fear of life in general, but it will take a long time.

F.H.: I agree, but only if the dog shows promise and if you can give the dog sufficient confidence to overcome his disabilities in a reasonable time. The main requirement is patience. Take the dog about with you, let it mix with the family – especially with children with whom it should be encouraged to play – let your wife take it out on a lead, and you take it into pubs if you go for a drink. However, if you have tried kindness and patience for a while and not succeeded, I would get rid of the dog.

10. The dog who is too biddable

PROBLEM: A fully trained dog, who has been over-trained and who is always asking for direction signals and if left on his own just sits and does nothing – he may even refuse to pick a dummy unless told to do so and may not come back unless signalled in.

F.H.: This fault is almost as bad as an over-confident dog and is extremely difficult to eradicate.

J.K.: I am very keen on early training in puppyhood, but this fault very often arises in early training. With a biddable dog the training must be confined to basic obedience and the emphasis placed on hunting and teaching him perseverance – direction signals should and must be left till later. Hunting is a natural instinct so that it does no harm to teach your puppy hunting, but if you give him direction signals and use the stop whistle too much at an early date you will curb his enthusiasm for hunting and make him too dependent on the trainer.

F.H.: The purpose of early training is to get the puppy going well. I even let some puppies chase. The fault is definitely due to over-training, either in puppyhood or at a later date. However, there are some dogs who seem to be naturally lazy and prefer *you* to find the game rather than hunt for themselves.

J.K.: It takes a lot of time to retrain such a dog – some trainers don't realize how long it takes to eradicate any fault – there are no instant cures in dog-training.

F.H.: The cure is to stop whistling and using hand signals – even cease using the stop whistle. He must have no unseen retrieves which would necessitate hand signals, but plenty of marked ones, preferably over hedges, so he has to be on his own and do some hunting. Walls should be used and woods; if he comes back he must be spoken to sharply and sent out again, but praised excessively if he finds. The main point is that he should be made to hunt out of sight of his handler, as if he can see you he will continue to ask for guidance. Take him out at dusk if you like, and he should have as much work in the shooting field as possible, also with other dogs so as to make him keen and jealous, but the handler should remember to keep his whistle in his pocket. He should not be trained daily but should be rested between sessions to make him keen and and speed him up.

J.K.: I agree, it is a terrible thing to have a too-biddable dog as half the time you don't know where the damned pheasant is yourself!

11. *The dog who is gun-nervous*

PROBLEM: A young dog when introduced to gunfire runs away and is obviously nervous even when a gun is brought near him.

F.H.: Gun-nervousness, which is relatively common to some degree in young dogs, must not be confused with gun-shyness for which there is no cure. A dog who is gun-nervous has probably been trained to the gun wrongly or frightened with a stick, brush or some other implement when young – a stick must never be used to chastise a dog as he may associate this with a gun. Apart from making him gun-nervous, he will be frightened on formal shooting days when beaters tap the bushes with their sticks. True gun-shyness is very rare and associated with a dog who is so nervous that he is untrainable anyway. A gun-shy dog

73

will take off into the blue if you pick up a gun, and not come back. If he finds his way home he will be shivering in the kennel and will take off again if he sees a gun. The same dog, however, will hunt well if there is nobody with a gun out with him.

J.K.: I was asked to look at a dog a little while ago whose master said he was gun-shy – admittedly the dog tried to run away when a gun was fired anywhere near him and was nervous and upset at the sight of a gun – but the dog was so stable otherwise, friendly to me and not in the least nervous, that I had no hesitation in saying that the dog was only gun-nervous, having been wrongly treated in some way, and could easily be cured – as was, in fact, proved in the next few weeks. I think that a dog should be introduced gradually to the gun at an early age and while he is feeding, so that he associates it with pleasure. Every dog should also be gradually accustomed to loud noise, such as beer bottles being thrown into bins in pubs; the dummy thrower also helps to accustom a dog to noise. It is also useful to allow a dog to sleep with the gun near him so that he gets used to the smell of it. If a dog is introduced to the gun properly there should be no problem as regards gun-nervousness.

F. H.: However, if a dog has become gun-nervous, I usually take the dog out with a friend and let the friend stand, say, 150 yards away with a .410 shotgun. When he discharges the gun, I give the dog a piece of meat – one should have a pocketful. If the dog shows fear of the noise I take him still further off from the noise, and upon each discharge of the gun, feed him a titbit. I continue this for a period of time, going ever nearer to the gun, and eventually he will tolerate the noise and the gun being thrown to the shoulder in anticipation of food – from thence throwing a dummy, firing a gun and allowing the dog to run in will probably complete the cure. There are only about three occasions

74

when I would use food as a means of training – I think in this case it is the easiest way, but it can be done by petting and coaxing, though it will probably take longer. Although the use of food will eliminate this fault it may cause a further fault in that the dog will look to the trainer for food when a gun is fired, thus taking his eye off the dummy or game and thereby not marking, but this would probably rectify itself as the dog gets keener and more confident.

J.K.: I am indeed glad to hear that you would consider the use of food even though you have qualified your statement, but I am a little disturbed that you allow the dog to run in. However, I know that your dogs are steady. But I wouldn't chance it myself. It is true that, if there is a continuous noise, after a time all animals ignore it – mowing the grass around the kennel is one instance; but noise could also be made by a loudspeaker playing pop music – this can be used to accustom a dog to a gun. While the continuous noise is being made a gun is fired at gradually decreasing distances from the dog. Another method is to interest the dog in a tame duck or dead or alive game – tease him with the game while a friend fires the gun. I think also that in gun training a dog should always be on a lead – to give him confidence and to prevent him getting away.

12. *The dog who lacks drive*

PROBLEM: A young dog of 10 months who appears to be completely uninterested in his work and does not show the normal enthusiasm of a dog of his age.

F.H.: This may be due to breeding. Show dogs, in a good many cases, have their natural instincts bred out of them, and it demonstrates the necessity of only training those dogs who have impeccable parents and grandparents, of field-trial stock, and whose performance in the field is known. Of course, there are the occasional throwbacks – or it may be due to too hard an upbringing as a small puppy. I would suggest giving the dog lots of freedom, relaxing discipline, particularly the stop whistle, and if necessary allowing it to chase a few rabbits in a wood with a fairly good bottom. This will most probably get it a little excited but it will often help to get the dog to face cover. It is much more likely to dash into cover after a rabbit than after a dummy at a wave of your hand.

J.K.: I never allow my dogs to chase as they may remember this at a later date, and if they do it it is hard to cure.

F.H.: I think it is the lesser of two evils, and I feel that it is easier to cure it of chasing at a later date, when it has become confident and wishes to hunt.

J.K.: Chasing is a very basic instinct, and I doubt if you ever repress the desire completely – admittedly if you encourage a young dog to chase, you will get a good-going dog.

F.H.: Rubbish! When the dog is mature I feel that I shall be able to control it – we are aiming for a good-going dog with drive.

J.K.: I would try to tease my dog, to get it excited, with possibly dead game. I would play with it, run away from it, to make it follow quickly; let it jump up at me, and let it play for long periods with other dogs. The importance of playing is often neglected. I would, in fact, do everything in my power to get it excited and interested, but not let it chase.

F.H.: Well, whatever happens, I shall get a dog with drive and you may not.

13. *The dog who is jealous*

PROBLEM: The dog who is so jealous that he won't let another dog approach his master – he is a fighter and snaps and snarls, and won't even let another dog go past him with a bird in his mouth without trying to take it from him.

J.K.: Jealousy manifests itself in many forms – an old bitch may be jealous of a young bitch – a bitch of mine only yipped if another dog was working directly in front of her, but not otherwise. Another dog I know would not let another handler and his dog approach her master at trials, and was a great nuisance in consequence. She was a completely one-man dog and would take no notice of any other person except that she had one friend, a girl who had brought her up as a puppy. A bitch just before her heat may become jealous, which she shows by either open antagonism or by sulking. Greyhounds are always muzzled when they race in case a jealous fight breaks out. I consider that emotional problems, being part of the animal's basic make-up, are very difficult to cure and are persistent, but the trainer should be able to some extent to keep them under control by discipline. Jealousy is usually associated with a difficult temperament, but not necessarily with a nervous one. The dogs are often highly intelligent but should be able to take a severe reprimand.

F.H.: This type of dog often makes a good guard or house dog, being very possessive. The trainer needs the help of friends to correct this fault. Sit the dog down on a lead and get your friends to walk their dogs past and around him, fairly close to him. If your dog growls or shows his teeth, or in any way offers to attack, bring a choke chain down sharply across his back. Keep this up until the dog sits quietly beside you, ignoring the other animals. Proceed from this by arranging for other dogs to retrieve across his front; if the dog shows any signs of jealousy, give it the same treatment as above and continue until it sits quietly beside you – this is really part of obedience training.

14. The dog who is untrainable

PROBLEM: A dog who has been under training for 2 months and is thought to be untrainable.

F.H.: I consider that almost any dog of any breed can be trained to do most things; some will obviously do it better than others. The only exception is a dog who is mentally unbalanced, and usually this becomes obvious fairly early in life, before too much time has been spent trying to train him. I have had two dogs who showed promise and then suddenly developed bizarre behaviour. On a post-mortem one of these showed a brain tumour; on the other no post mortem was performed.

J.K.: There are many dogs, however, who although trainable are not worth training owing to some fault through temperamental or physical disability.

(1) There is the dog who is too nervous to train satisfactorily, although I would probably persevere with this type longer than you would.

(2) There is the really brash dog, but he has to be also dishonest before I would discard him; and youthful exuberance must be distinguished from the dog who won't look at his master or try to please him.

(3) There is also the stupid dog who appears not to have the necessary instincts (he runs around and takes no interest in his job, possibly won't even go out to a seen retrieve) – I think I would discard him at a very early date.

If we now consider the faults:

(4) There is the yipper – I consider this can be suspected at a very early date, and only gets worse. He must be discarded very early indeed.

(5) The hard-mouthed dog – he must be distinguished from a dog who refuses to let go of the dummy: and before getting rid of him I would make sure that he had crushed a couple of birds.

(6) The truly gun-shy dog.

Then of the physical disabilities, there are:

(7) The mentally unbalanced dog.

(8) The epileptic.

(9) The dog who has hereditary blindness.

(10) A dog who has hip dysplasia.

I have never met a dog who can't scent, except in one case where the dog was working while he had a mild distemper infection. It was interesting to watch and proved how little dogs depend on their eyesight.

F.H.: In most cases, I think that it should be possible to tell whether a dog is worth training within three months of owning him – if he is not, the sooner the dog is discarded the better, or if the dog is not yours, the owner should be informed. Unfortunately, as hope springs eternal in the human heart we tend to persevere and only suffer for our optimism.

Perversions

15. The dog who eats faeces

PROBLEM: The young dog who persists in eating (a) the faeces of cattle and sheep and (b) his own faeces.

J.K. The normal way of feeding in the wild is for the wolf or wild dog first to rip open the animal's stomach and to eat the liver and intestines before going on to muscles and then finally bones. Thus, by eating half-digested vegetable residue in the intestines he gains a valuable source of vitamins and must also, at the same time, eat a certain amount of faeces.

There is a story about this which is amusing:

King James I of England, who was also King James VI of Scotland, was a highly intelligent man who suffered from wretched health. He drooled and slobbered his way through life supported on both sides by two handsome youths, for whom he had a great partiality, and he used them also as crutches, for his feet and legs hurt him cruelly. However, he could sit up on a horse and hunt. At times, after he had killed a hart he would cause the huntsmen to open up its belly and, sitting upon a convenient stone and having removed his boots, would thrust his naked feet into the entrails as he found the warmth soothing to him and of great curative value. After a time his youths would help him again upon his horse and he would go home greatly comforted, whereupon the huntsmen would let the hounds eat the entrails which the King had sanctified, as was the custom in those days.

F.H.: I also think that a labrador's greatest instinct and pleasure is to carry things in his mouth – if he starts carrying faeces he will soon swallow some.

J.K.: Dogs judge their food principally by smell. They bolt their food and taste is only a secondary consideration – one reason why it is easy to poison a dog. They certainly don't mind the smell of faeces – they have no inhibitions, as we have.

F.H.: In the case of their own faeces, they probably dislike the taste, but if they are shut up in kennels for a long time they get bored, carry their own faeces about and finally start eating them, having got used to the taste.

J.K.: In the case of the faeces of sheep and cattle, you often see a dog licking a cowpat. It is very irritating to see a dog pick up faeces when he is hunting for a dummy, or for that matter sheep's faeces when at heel; in fact, the habit is very common, but with the usual reprimand the dogs seem to grow out of it as they grow older.

F.H.: Even if you correct their diet and give plenty of vitamins, especially B and C – the vitamins principally con-

tained in vegetable matter – once the habit of eating faeces
has been established they continue to eat them, unless
cured in other ways.

J.K.: I don't suppose this has any bearing on the discussion,
but human lunatics sometimes eat their own faeces!

F.H.: The cure is to correct any errors of diet and to increase
the amount given so that they don't get hungry, to leave
some hard bones in their kennels with which they can
occupy their time by gnawing, and to act as a toy for them
to carry about, as well as the usual reprimand when out
training.

J.K.: As a matter of fact, if you can train your dogs to go out
and defecate after every meal so that the kennels are never
fouled, and with most of my dogs I manage this, I don't
think the problem will arise.

I have read that in America they sometimes instal a
continuous food dispenser, like a hopper, so that the dog
can take a mouthful of food when he likes. The food is
purposely made monotonous and apparently the dogs soon
cease over-eating. Apparently dogs fed this way do not
over-eat. Also they have tried putting the dogs' faeces on a
metal plate attached to a shock machine, but apparently the
latter method is not only complicated but also not very
successful.

16. The dog who eats rubbish

PROBLEM: Some dogs have the objectionable habit of eating
carrion or any filth however 'high' it is.

J.K.: The normal eating habit of a dog is to eat meat which is
slightly 'high'. There comes a stage, however, when the
food is too 'high' for the dog and is rejected. After the
Second World War, when meat was difficult to obtain and I
had no refrigerator for dog food, I used to buy meat in

quantity and bury it so that, although it got a little 'high',
it did not go rotten.

F.H.: A dog is still interested in the smell of very 'high',
carrion even if he won't eat it, and after smelling it may either roll on it or bring it back as a present
to you.

J.K.: A wolf will move his den and his puppies when it has
become befouled with regurgitated food and the remains of
carcasses that have gone past the point of no recall. I think
myself, however, that it is probably not the stench which
drives him away but the myriad flies which make his life
unbearable.

F.H.: It comes back to the fact that dogs judge palatability
by smell rather than by taste and dogs are very catholic in
their ideas of which smells are pleasant.

J.K.: In one way, however, dogs are conservative. If a dog
has never been fed on meat, for example, he will reject it
until he has acquired the taste for it by carrying it in his
mouth, and a dog will not eat the flesh of another
dog.

F.H.: If a dog has acquired the taste for carrion, his diet
should be attended to.

Faults when out

17. The dog who cannot mark

PROBLEM: Some dogs are good markers, others never acquire
this attribute. How can the handler help a poor marker?

J.K.: Marking is an acquired attribute bred into the dog by a
few generations of training. I do not believe that marking is
an instinctive characteristic. No bird in the natural state
falls out of the sky and lies dead on the ground for the dog
to pick – so marking has to be taught.

A Dialogue on Difficulties

F.H.: I think a dog who is a really good marker is born, not made – like a good shot. Some dogs are really exceptional and these make the retrieving of walked-up game look easy and make the job of handling and whistling unnecessary in many cases. They seem to be capable of marking game down in really heavy cover and thick roots, which from their position near the ground is really uncanny. Sometimes they are helped by hearing a thump on the ground but not always. Some dogs can do multiple marks and remember the one which has not been picked – and often they take their eyes off a mark or are moved but still remember where the game lies.

J.K.: The brash dog overmarks through too much enthusiasm – this can be controlled by giving shorter marks. The overtrained dog who is too biddable and depends too much on his handler may become too lazy to mark and must be retrained. In training to mark there are certain practices which are not helpful – for example, the use of white dummies. Also, it is not helpful to use the dummy thrower too often from heel. Wherever possible the dummy should be thrown as a crossing shot, which makes it far easier for the dog. In training a dog to mark, the dummy should at first be thrown only a short distance on a plain field, the distance being gradually increased. Following this, short marks into light cover where the dog can find the dummy as soon as he arrives in the area. Only at a very late stage should markings be tried over hedges and in difficult cover. In teaching to mark, the trainer always wants the dog to find the dummy immediately he is in the area. If he does not do so he should be allowed to work out the problem for himself and the trainer should, within reason, refrain from whistling and signalling. Another useful exercise when there is a field of grass is for the trainer to put up his dog, walk out 50 yards or so and throw the dummy up into the air, then walk back and send his dog out. The dog has a double track to follow – he is thus taught to run out straight – he has marked the dummy and he finds it immediately.

F.H.: I think that by careful and patient training you can improve a dog's marking ability, but I don't think you will ever *make* a brilliant marker. I would suggest that you go with a friend and stand about 30 to 40 yards apart on a pasture field; each of you in turn throw a dummy well into the air, at the same time shouting the dog's name in order to attract its attention. This done fairly regularly should help, but like all training methods must not be done too often or the animal becomes bored. It is also helpful to fire a dummy from a trainer across the front of the dog, while it is sitting, at a range of about 15 yards, bouncing the dummy on the ground so that the dog may become interested and keep his eyes on it.

J.K.: One last thought on marking – whether your dog is a good marker or a bad one, do try to send your dog from heel down-wind of the mark. Even the best dogs may miss it if they pass it up-wind.

18. The dog who takes off into the blue

PROBLEM: A 2-year-old trained dog performs well at medium distances but, if he is too far out or not in sight of his handler, takes off and goes wherever he wishes.

F.H.: They are always brash good-going dogs. The biddable dog either loses confidence in these circumstances and sits, or he comes back towards his handler to ask for directions.

J.K.: I think the cause is twofold. First, being a brash, good-going dog he has probably been severely disciplined under training. When he gets away from his handler he feels that he is free and starts to enjoy himself doing whatever he thinks best. He may find a hare track which he wants to follow. He is, I think, a somewhat dishonest type of dog who does not wish to please his handler and will be always ready to challenge the latter's authority. Secondly, there has been a breakdown in the training schedule. One of the objects of training is to establish far-distance obedience. I think the trainer should take the dog back to first principles: he should practise endlessly direction signals – 'find the lady' exercise, with three dummies at right angles and the dog between them, the trainer directing the dog at distances up to 125 yards. At every disobedience of a signal, the handler must go out to the dog and reprimand him. This should be kept up for at least three weeks. The dog must learn that he can't get away with disobedience at this distance. The dog should never be allowed to hunt out of sight, where the handler cannot see what he is up to, unless the handler has a friend with him to watch the dog.

F.H.: The reason for this fault is probably that the dog is more interested in hunting than he is in you. He gets his nose down and just hunts on regardless of whistle or voice. When the dog has been properly trained to the stop whistle, if he doesn't stop on command he is wilfully disobedient and the trainer must get after him and bring him back to the spot where he was when he blew the whistle. He must be soundly berated, and on any subsequent occasion, when he fails to stop, must be chastised as near as possible to the place where he sinned. The dog must be made to obey the whistle. Subsequently when he gets hunting too far away from the bird, if he is obedient his head can be lifted and the dog brought back to the area in which you require him to hunt.

J.K.: I think that the American electric collar, if used properly when the dog has been given due warning and has disobeyed, might be useful here to persuade the dog that distance does not make him immune from punishment.

19. *The dog who runs in or chases*

PROBLEM: A trained dog who runs in or chases on more than one occasion.

J.K.: Both running in and chasing when out are the same fault and the dog is giving in to a primary instinct and refusing to accept discipline.

FH.: It can happen with a rather wild, headstrong dog and it can also happen to a dog with whom you have had to be rather gentle in training, a dog upon whom you could put very little pressure lest you inhibit him – the kind of animal which will dry up if you take a firm line. But if he runs in or chases he has evidently become keen and steps have to be taken to prevent this very serious fault.

J.K.: I can remember three interesting examples of running in. The first was on a run-off at a trial, so the dog must have done good work. A pheasant fell some distance out and the dog slowly walked in, in spite of the lamentations and shouts of his handler; he picked the pheasant and then walked back to deliver, all in slow motion.

The second example was in a trial: my dog was getting more and more excited and prancing – I kept looking at the other handler's dog who was very placid and keeping strictly to heel and thinking: If only I had a dog like that how pleasant it would be! Suddenly a pheasant fell in front of us; my dog remained steady, the other dog went out like a shot from a gun and collected the bird. I spoke later to the handler, who was a professional, and he said that the dog had done this before. I think this points the moral that, once a dog starts running in, it is very difficult to curb and appearances are often deceptive.

The third case was my own dog who ran in after a hare. When I eventually got her back I gave the dog a really severe hiding. I was just picking up my gun when, as often happens, another hare got up. When I finally retrieved my dog for the second time, I decided not to punish her severely twice in one day, so I put her to heel. I ran that dog in trials and shot over her for five years and she never again ran in until she was 9 years old, when to my surprise she ran in after a duck I had shot. I think this last run in was possibly caused by my relaxing discipline; also an old dog does tend to revert to puppyhood, as do humans to childhood. It demonstrates, however, that a primary instinct is never lost.

F.H.: I saw a dog once who was being held by his handler struggle free and actually catch a hare which was passing in front of him.

J.K.: The treatment is well known and if you can't cure the fault the dog must be got rid of. The handler must be able to trust his dog, but this does not mean that he mustn't at all times keep an eye on him. There's nothing more wearying than waiting for a dog to run in and trying to prevent it.

F.H.: If the dog breaks heel to run in, he can often be stopped by the trainer anticipating his action, which he should try to do on every occasion by bringing a strap or choke chain sharply down across the dog's back as he leaves heel. Alternatively a light nylon cord can be fastened round the dog's neck, the trainer lays about 10 yards on the grass and wraps the other end firmly round his hand in order not to get burned by the cord slipping. When the dog runs in and reaches the end of the slack cord, he is firmly jerked so that he lands on his back. The very shaken dog is then dragged back to the spot where he broke heel, and soundly berated. If the dog chases when far out hunting, the trainer must go out and catch the dog, drag it back to the place where the chase commenced and chastise it thoroughly. He must be very firm but just to get this obedience.

Cattle training

20. *The dog who is afraid of cattle and livestock*

PROBLEM: Some dogs will circle widely to avoid a flock of sheep and many dogs show nervousness when cattle come up around them snorting and butting.

J.K.: Dogs should be trained to livestock at a very early age. A young puppy can be introduced to calves and also allowed to smell at cows with a gate between them. Sheep are really no problem – it is usually a question of preventing the dog chasing them. One of my older dogs would even run over the backs of sheep in a pen.

F.H.: It is really most nerve-wracking for any dog to be in a field full of heifers or bullocks. In fact, it is not only dogs who are nervous of cattle!

J.K.: In a trial I had to run my dog among some bullocks after a runner. The dog did not find. The next competitor said to the judges that he was afraid that his dog would not face the cattle. The judge quite rightly said, 'Well, the first dog faced them – if you don't wish to send your dog that is, of course, up to you.'

F.H.: I find the best idea is to take two or three dogs, probably one of them old and experienced, into a field where there are cattle, and sit on a shooting-stick with all the dogs on leads. You don't need to go near the livestock, they will soon come to the dogs. Talk to the dogs and try to soothe them, and the presence of the older animal, who will ignore the snorts of the cattle, will help to reassure the younger dogs. This will have to be repeated on many occasions until eventually the dogs will even snap at the cattle if they approach. This should be encouraged because the cattle will back off and this will reassure the dog that they are harmless. Be careful, however, not to let a bullock butt your dog.

21. The dog who won't hunt

PROBLEM: An 18-months-old dog who runs about aimlessly and does not hunt with style.

J.K.: Hunting is, after all, a natural instinct, and if lacking it is a very annoying fault, usually indicating a worthless dog. Style in hunting is the first quality I look for in buying a small pup.

F.H.: Hunting should be taught from very early puppyhood with the exercise of trying to make the puppy hunt in a circle around you with the ball only a short distance away. Hunting is the most important part of training and every effort must be made to make your dog a good and systematic hunter and also to persevere in his hunting.

J.K.: A very biddable dog will lack perseverance if he has been over-trained. Too many signals tend to suppress the hunting instinct in such a dog. Whatever the cause, the handler has to do all the work and handle the dog on to the bird. Amateur trainers seem always to want to find the dummy. One of the most important rules of training is to let the dog work it out for himself, however long it takes.

F.H.: To improve an over-biddable dog's hunting ability he should be hunted over a wall or on the other side of a hedge, and if he looks to the handler for instructions the handler turns his back on him. If the dog appears to be taking no interest in his job, a good shake will improve things considerably.

J.K.: I agree. I think you can also improve a lazy dog by using dead game and whenever he flags make encouraging noises, perhaps waste a cartridge or two to increase the excitement; but if these measures fail it must be remembered that disinterested hunting is still disobedience and the dog should be punished.

There is one other exercise you can try on a young dog. It is possible to take a page from spaniel training and place an unseen dummy at some distance away. Make your dog traverse backwards and forwards in front of you as you advance towards the dummy and finally stop a few yards off so that the dog can find it easily, but after it has hunted a considerable area of ground. You have thus been near the dog all the time and have encouraged it to go on hunting.

22. The dog who won't face cover – nettles

PROBLEM: An 18-months-old dog who won't go through a hedge without running up and down to find a gap; also he won't push his way into a patch of brambles. There is also the problem of the dog who won't face nettles.

F.H.: Most of these dogs lack drive, but it has to be proved to them in training that the hedge and ditch can be got through, that the brambles are not so bad, and that a nettle gives rise to only slight discomfort. If as a pup a dog is allowed plenty of freedom, and taken into woods and grass, he will most probably go pushing into briars after rabbits. This can be corrected later when real training starts, but his willingness to face cover will have become a habit.

J.K.: Some dogs seem to suffer from nettles much more than others. My present dog never seems to notice them at all. Another dog I know rolls and rubs himself if he gets near a nettle. It is very annoying if a dog runs up and down a hedge to find an easy gap to get through. I always see that it is possible to get through and then I stop him and push him through – if he hesitates on the way back, I again stop him and call him in. On the whole, however, if he has gone through one way, he will tend to come back the same route, unless there is a gate or a much easier hole. I gradually increase the difficulties until he learns to push his way through. If I am in trouble I stand over him and push him through. In the same way with brambles: I put the ball in the middle, but where it is possible for him to get it, and let him see me do it – or at least arrange that he can scent it with the wind in the right direction. I then give him time to work it out for himself. If he doesn't find, I again stand over him and push him through the bramble bush. If I am sure that he knows where the ball is, but won't face the brambles, I give him a shake so that he knows he must not disobey.

F.H.: A dog who will not face brambles can be trained by being left without food for a day, then taken out once you have filled your pocket full of pieces of meat. Throw the meat, a piece at a time, into cover – sparse cover at first and then more punishing cover as the pupil responds. The same treatment applies to nettles, but give the dog the wind so that he knows where the meat is, close to the edge at first and then deeper in the bed, as the dog becomes bolder.

23. *The dog who won't face water*

PROBLEM: A dog who, having been adequately trained and encouraged to swim, still refuses to enter water and is frightened of it.

F.H.: It is most unusual to find any four-legged animal who can't swim. It is mostly a matter of patience and perseverance to get any dog into water; in the majority of cases it presents no problem.

J.K.: Labradors, who came from Newfoundland and were mostly fishermen's dogs, have an inherited love of water and I agree it is rare to have any difficulty. Golden retrievers have not the inherited instinct to this extent, and there may be difficulty at times. Some dogs are 'water dogs'; others are not. All dogs will paddle, but some will only swim if they have to.

F.H.: Should a dog be loath to enter water, it is advisable to pick a hot day and, taking two or three dogs with you, exercise them in a field near the river. When they are hot and panting, take them to the river and choose as your spot a shallow sloping bank and shallow water. Send the dogs out to play and the older dogs will rush to the water for a drink and swim. The dogs you are training will not want to be left and will probably join them, and once it becomes a familiar element, it isn't long before each will swim and enter on command. Or you may walk across a river, leaving the dogs sitting on the other side, then call them to you – and your dog will probably follow the others.

J.K.: I think the real problem arises with a dog who has not been trained as a young puppy, say 9 months old. In our problem dog all these exercises and many more had been tried without success. It seems unnecessary to say that this type of dog must never be 'thrown in at the deep end'.

F.H.: If these tactics fail you can carry the dog into water, coaxing and petting him with a lead on his neck. Place him in the water and let him swim around you, supporting his head above the water with the lead and collar (not a choke chain), but try not to let him panic. Or, if you have access to a boat, you can take it out on a lake and let the dog swim beside the boat. As a last resort, the trainer takes a light but strong cane or pole, attaches this to the dog's collar and walks him first in the shallows, keeping him in the water with the pole, and then along the bank into deeper water where the dog has to swim a pole's length away. These latter methods are rather forceful and it is very unlikely that they will ever be required, but they do work in many cases. A dog who has been trained from generations of working parents invariably takes to water and, in fact, it is usually more trouble getting him out and keeping him out than getting him in.

24. *The dog who won't jump with a dummy*

PROBLEM: A 9-months-old dog who retrieved well and could jump; but whenever he had anything in his mouth he would refuse to jump up even a small bank.

J.K.: Many dogs jump better free than when carrying a dummy – and it is almost normal when you are training, for a dog to refuse a difficult jump if holding something in his mouth. This dog had the trait to an abnormal degree.
F.H.: This, I would think, is purely due to lack of confidence, provided it will jump with its mouth empty.
J.K.: To build up this confidence, I would practise jumping endlessly – walls, wire, banks, rails, without a dummy, until the dog is a really good jumper. Then start him jumping small jumps carrying a tennis ball which has no weight. If I still had difficulty, I would put him on a lead, and jump small jumps with him. I don't think that there is a big problem here.

Golden retriever in action – jumping a bank

F.H.: I would take a small dummy and a very small fence and encourage him with an older dog – walk away, calling the dogs to you; if the fence is small enough he will just hop over it. The dog is then praised profusely when he reaches you. Gradually raise the fence until the animal has complete confidence. Should this fail, you can place the dog on one side of the fence, and position yourself on the other; put a choke chain on the dog with a strong lead attached and, as you give the order 'over', encourage the dog by giving a jerk on the lead. If he refuses to jump you can even lift him over with the lead – after a few lessons he will get the idea to jump on command.

94

25. *The dog who blinks a bird*

PROBLEM: It is suspected that a half-trained dog who has found a bird, instead of picking it, continues to hunt the area with great enthusiasm.

J.K.: The type of dog who may blink a bird is usually brash and dishonest. He would rather hunt than retrieve and does not wish to please his handler. One of the difficulties is that the handler is never quite sure whether the dog has blinked the bird or just not found. I was third dog down in a trial and my dog was hunting all round a dead pheasant. One of the judges said to the other, 'I think that dog has blinked the bird.' The other judge said, 'I know that dog. He has never blinked a bird in his life and never will.' Just then my dog got a whiff of the pheasant and picked it – one can never be sure of the vagaries of scent or whether the bird may be in a hole.

F.H.: The experienced handler should be able to tell if his dog has scented a bird by the dog whipping round, by the movements of his tail and by his ears going up.

J.K.: If you suspect a dog of blinking, you must go out and assure yourself that the bird is in full sight.

F.H.: All you can do, if you have decided that the bird has been blinked, is to chastise the dog, stuff the bird in its mouth and make it bring the bird to you. Then throw the bird out and make the dog retrieve it. The following day the lesson can be duplicated, preferably in interesting cover and with dummies – if he blinks birds when other scents are about, he will most probably blink dummies.

J.K.: A dog with this fault can never be trusted completely – or completely cured because he will do it when he is out of sight or in a wood.

F.H.: We are completely agreed that a dog who has been proved to have this fault should be got rid of.

26. *The dog who won't look at the handler*

PROBLEM: An 18-months-old dog still will not look at his handler for direction signals.

F.H.: Possibly this problem would not arise with a very young puppy which you have brought up yourself and which is used to watching you.

J.K.: It is usually found in an independent dog who will rely on no one but himself.

F.H.: This is a very irritating fault in a brash dog who will probably stop on the stop whistle but then prefers to sniff the air around him and see what is going on, rather than look towards the handler. Such dogs will, of course, never stop of their own accord and ask for directions.

J.K.: It is very difficult to train a dog who refuses to look at you. If you 'hup' him and wait till he looks at you, you may have to wait a very long time and exercise a great deal of patience. The first sign of successful training is when the dog does start looking back towards the trainer.

F.H.: Train the dog with him very near you, only very gradually extending the distance between you and your dog, with a good shake every time he starts looking round, if calling his name has failed to get his attention. His temperament is probably wrong and it will be best to get rid of the dog.

27. *The dog who refuses to stay on the drop, or who creeps*

PROBLEM: A dog of any age who refuses to stay still on the drop, often a real fast good-going dog.

F.H.: He is often a keen, eager type of beast, often a real fast good-going dog.

J.K.: I think this usually occurs when other dogs are present, and the trainer has lost concentration on his dog, and allows it – either because he is talking to other people, or watching other people's dogs. It seldom occurs in the shooting field or trial because the dog is very interested in what is going on.

F.H.: He needs firm handling and once you have put him down you must insist he stays there. If he creeps or moves at all, you take hold of him by the scruff of the neck and put him back, in no uncertain manner, to the place where he ought to to be. Once a dog has been put down or whistled to stop, you must insist that he obeys every order that is given. The golden rule is: 'Never give the order if you are not in a position to enforce it.'

J.K.: This fault should be checked from the very beginning, so that it does not become a habit. If you have a creeper, make him sit rather than lie down – give him exercises in sitting when there are no distractions and keep him sitting for five to ten minutes before letting him go and play. Firmly reprimand him, as Frank says, at the least move.

28. The dog who picks up badly

PROBLEM: A young dog who takes a long time picking up game – mouthing it, putting it down, perhaps turning it over before before taking a firm grip and bringing it to hand.

J.K.: This fault is always found in soft-mouthed, sensitive dogs. The brash dog strikes at the game, takes a firm grip and scoops it up. It is possibly also found in rather immature dogs who want to play with the game.

F.H.: I consider that this fault may be made worse by the trainer who tries to hurry his dog by whistling him in before he has got a good grip of the bird, thus distracting his attention.

J.K.: I agree. I had a dog with this fault and tried to cure him by telling him to 'bring it on'. He knew by the tone of my voice that he was doing something wrong and became even more uncertain.

F.H.: All dogs have to learn how to pick up the various types of game. Pheasants are difficult compared to ducks and the game may be in any position. Many dogs are suspicious at first of wounded game – so the dog must be given plenty of practice. Once he has learnt to collect wounded game, picking it improves his performance as the added excitement and the possibility of the game moving teaches him to strike at it quickly.

J.K.: It is permissible for a dog who is soft-mouthed, having failed to get a grip on a hare, to pick it up by the skin of the back and bring it in, as long as he does it expeditiously and does not continually put it down. It is also permissible for a dog to put game down once to get a better grip.

F.H.: This is a rather difficult fault to cure, but some improvement may be gained by throwing the game only a short distance away and, after sending your dog, run away from him so as to make him want to speed up the pick-up.

J.K.: I also think that heavy dummies up to 5lb and dummies half filled with sand so that they are awkward to carry should be used in training.

F.H.: Failing these measures the dog may be force-trained to pick up quickly. The force method can be used on sensitive dogs – and the method is as follows. Have the dog in a confined space and throw the dummy a yard or two. If the dog fails to pick up quickly and neatly, force the dog's mouth open by pressing its lips against its teeth, and force the dummy into its mouth. Do this roughly so that it causes maximum discomfort and then tell the dog to hold. After this has been repeated several times, the dog will even snatch at the dummy, if you are holding it and say 'hie lost', in order to avoid the discomfort of having his mouth forced open. From this, it is a question of extending the distance and using game instead of dummies.

Retrieving

29. The dog who won't pick game or a dummy unless the handler's scent is upon it

PROBLEM: A 12-months-old dog who had been trained by his own master refused, when trained with other handlers, to pick anything unless it had the master's scent upon it.

J.K.: This is an extraordinary and rare fault – it is the nature of retrievers to pick and carry and I can't imagine what is the basic cause.

F.H.: He was a good, stylish, biddable dog and not nervous. I had trained him myself and I have no idea how this fault arose. I can't think of anything I did which might have been the cause. As you know, I do think that most faults in dogs are the result of either a bad upbringing or bad training, and invariably if you know the reason for a dog developing a fault it is much easier to take steps to rectify it, rather than to hazard a guess as to what may have caused the fault, possibly come up with the wrong answer and then proceed to a course of correction which may not get the desired result. I think that the first step in trying to correct this fault is probably to get clean dummies and use rubber gloves, and even handle the dummies with tongs so as to avoid all possible ways of getting your scent on the object to be retrieved. You should have discovered this fault when the dog is fairly young, so throw the clean dummy and let the dog run in. When he puts his head down to pick it, run away from him, calling his name, and try to get him to come back with the dummy before he has time to think. After a time if this exercise does not work, then you will have to go out to him and place the dummy in his mouth and make him carry it back alongside you. If he won't do this and spits out the dummy, then a course of forced retrieving is called for – this is what I would do. However, the mere mention of forced retrieving has J.K. up in arms and giving me a lecture on positive and negative training! I was initiated into dog-training in an era when there was no one to ask advice from and I had to learn the hard way. My father trained setters and my uncle sheep dogs and their rule was quite simple – if the dogs wouldn't do it, they were made to. To some degree they were severe to obtain an end. Methods of training these days are very much more gentle, and I would think better. I have known both sides – having seen dogs broken to the gun rather than trained to the gun.

J.K.: The dog was a good one – so finally you trained it by force methods. What happened to the dog in the end?

F.H.: I was to a large degree successful and ran him in trials, one of which the dog won. However, following that he blinked a bird so I got rid of him.

30. *The dog who drops the bird*

PROBLEM: A trained dog who puts the game down on more than one occasion on the way in from a retrieve.

F.H.: The dog who puts the bird down on return quite often has a very soft mouth. It lifts the bird tenderly and carries it loosely. This you won't see in a dog who has been trained by the forced method. It is a slovenly, untidy habit and shouldn't be tolerated. It is permissible for a dog to put a bird or a hare down on one occasion to get a better grip; but I think a repeat performance is a serious fault.

J.K.: They seldom do it with live birds, although one of my dogs put a live partridge down on three occasions on the way in – luckily the bird did not fly away. Nor do they put the bird down when they stop to defecate – although this has happened on one occasion that I saw. I was severely criticized when, at the beginning of the season, my dog put a hare down two or three times on the way in. Knowing the dog, I said, 'I don't think she will do it again' – this was true until years later she was sent out for a wounded and kicking hare and I had the greatest trouble in persuading her to bring it in at all. She had, in fact, never picked a wounded hare – so this last failure was really my fault in that when she was fully trained and experienced I should have given her one.

F.H.: I have seen these very soft-mouthed dogs have the bird knocked out of their mouths when forcing their way through kale. On the other hand, a dog who jumps in and strikes has a fair chance of damaging the game.

J.K.: A dog who puts the bird down when coming out of water in order to shake himself should be reprimanded, the bird thrown out and the dog made to bring it to hand properly. The dog who drops the bird just before delivery may have had the bird snatched off him by the handler: on one occasion a dog ran in and caught a hare and brought it to hand. The handler was seen belabouring the dog with the hare – I doubt if that dog delivered properly for a very long time and certainly not hares.

These two last examples of putting the game down at the handler's feet should be cured reasonably easily by correcting one's own faults and speaking sternly to the dog.

F.H.: If a dog has not been cured of dropping the game on the way in by reprimand, going out to him and making him pick it up and carry it, there is another method. I have heard of two dogs who were cured of this annoying habit by lashing a dead pheasant in their mouths and walking them round a field for about ten minutes two or three times a day. This, of course, is a form of forcing or making a dog do it.

I feel sure that you could also get success by forced retrieving, which is really making the dog frightened to drop it. I do think that there are occasions when forced retrieving can possibly cause a dog to squeeze a bird. Suppose a dog trained by forced retrieves has jumped a fence and the jolt on landing has loosened the dog's hold, then he will be more inclined to squeeze the harder to prevent it falling from his mouth rather than to put it down and take another grip. If you do have to force retrieve a dog, you get him where he can't get away from you; have the dummy in one hand and twist his ear with the other, at the same time placing your foot on his toes. When he opens his mouth, as he will do, press the dummy into his mouth and immediately release the pressure from his toes and his ears and pat him and talk to him. If he tries to spit out the dummy and drops it, the whole thing is repeated until, after a period of time, the dog will lift his head and take the dummy from your hand and pick it up from the ground after being told 'Hie lost'.

Forced retrieving is very controversial. One professional trainer said to me that you are apt to cause more faults than you put right. If you have a large enough kennel, it is better to discard a dog who won't retrieve or is a bad retriever, but if you are stuck with the dog I think that forcing is a more certain cure than spending weeks or possibly months trying to cajole the dog to return, and even then not being successful. One very good argument against the method is that if a retriever has to be forced to retrieve, it is better to discard the dog.

31. The dog who won't come back to the handler unless he has something in his mouth

PROBLEM: A fully trained dog who, although not being 'out of control', is very loath to come back to the handler when recalled.

F.H.: I don't think this is a very serious fault. No handler is overjoyed when his dog returns without having found a bird, but provided the dog is obedient to the whistle, he should and will come back on being recalled. I think it might be worth quoting Tom Southworth: 'If he fills his mouth he'll come back. If he doesn't, I don't want him back' – very true, and said with feeling.

J.K.: I agree it is hardly a fault. I use the same signal when moving the dog towards me while hunting and also to call him back to hand, except that I put more emphasis on the recall and repeat more often. It is not unreasonable, therefore, to expect him to come in, in short bursts, and hunt all the way in. Also, it is a good quality in a dog once he is told to hunt to show dash and perseverance – a quality some of our dogs have lost. If you wish to recall your dog, you must 'hup' him first, then, after due pause to enable him to calm down a little, call him in. So, as long as the dog obeys the whistle, I do not criticize him for slowness and certainly do not punish him. If, however, he takes no notice whatsoever of the whistle, this is a dog who is completely out of hand and it is another situation altogether. It is an eliminating fault. We have all been sorry for the handlers at trials who have to go out after their dogs – and this situation must be not only severely dealt with but also demands the retraining of the dog.

32. The dog who returns slowly when carrying game

PROBLEM: A trained dog who, after having found game, dawdles on the way back.

J.K.: Some dogs come back to you slowly and without dash even when they are not hunting and not carrying a bird. This is bad training. The dog should want to come back to you when he is called in, to get his petting. I was asked the other day why my dog returned so readily to me, and I said, with truth: practice and praise. However, there is the dog who returns slowly when he has a bird in his mouth. Occasionally he may smell a scent and stop to investigate. He is, of course, allowed to defecate or pass urine. Training consists of teaching your dog to ignore scents on the way out (a puppy never does). This should help him to ignore scents on the way back – and in all training he should be encouraged to return quickly, by whistling him in, calling to him and patting him in. However, if the problem arises, it is a difficult fault to cure. The trainer can't punish him for dawdling except by voice. I suppose in the end you have to get him into the habit of coming back quickly when he has nothing in his mouth and hope he learns from this.

F.H.: Time and patience may improve the dawdling habit. I don't think that a handler can do much more than encourage the dog to hurry back by voice, and whistle, or turn round and run away from him, because a dog does not like to be left behind. It may be possible to improve matters if you take out another dog with him, sit them both down 100 yards away and whistle them both to you, making a great fuss of the one that reaches you first and ignoring the other. Jealousy is a trait that can be used in many ways in training and quite often proves successful.

In General

33. On the differences between training retrievers and spaniels

J.K.: We must first establish that both breeds are trained in the same manner except for quartering and dropping to shot.

F.H.: I agree. Both breeds have to be steady at heel and when out; they have to hunt, swim, jump and retrieve smartly; and they have to respond to the same whistles and signals.

A Dialogue on Difficulties

Steady when out

J.K.: There is, however, a difference in the way they hunt – a spaniel is a 'hedgerow dog', who hunts closely; he is a bustling little dog who is not at his best on long retrieves. He should quest his ground about 15 to 20 yards out on either side of his handler, he should go with speed and style, yet cover his ground thoroughly. It is a cardinal sin if game is put up behind him; he should be willing and eager to face the roughest and most punishing cover; he must be taught to drop to shot and to flush and he must be steady at all times in the face of great temptation.

F.H.: Instinctively he is a hunter of cover and he is small enough to do this more satisfactorily than a labrador or other pure retriever. It is my opinion that too much emphasis is placed upon a spaniel doing long retrieves – probably owing to the shortage of rabbits. Long retrieves are the job of the retriever. A little slackness in retrieving is forgivable, provided he covers his ground well and goes with pace. In fact, if he has too many long retrieves he may tend to get too far out and his quartering ability may be diminished. It is as well to have two words of command: one if the dog is sent out to quarter and another if he is sent out after dead or wounded game – he soon learns the difference.

J.K.: To train a spaniel to drop to shot, he is first trained to sit to command and hand signals. Then the whistle is used until he drops to a whistle when no signal or command is given. After the association is established, a whistle is given and a cap pistol is fired at the same time. Finally it is only a small step for him to drop when a game gun is used.

F.H.: Questing is taught in several ways – it is advisable to be able to turn your dog with two short blasts of the whistle, but first, as in all training, he must be taught hand signals; and in the beginning both are used in combination. Also in the early stages the handler can walk from side to side with his dog, encouraging him to turn when he turns; but this must be stopped as soon as the dog has the idea of what is required of him – as, with a trained dog, the handler should walk in a straight line behind his dog, letting the dog cover the ground. The trainer can be helped if he has the use of a largish paddock about 30 yards wide; he walks down the middle, gives the order to turn when the dog reaches the wall on one side and then repeats it when he reaches the wall on the other. The trainer may also find the use of a check cord helpful to restrain the dog when he has reached the limit of the beat. Then with a wave of the arm and a signal he can be encouraged to hunt in the opposite direction.

J.K.: There are four points which I would like to emphasize. First, all questing should be taught up-wind as this keeps the dog nearer the handler and makes it easier for him to find. Secondly, an occasional dummy should be placed out so that the dog may have a retrieve. Thirdly, spaniels may get so keen on hunting they they might learn to blink a retrieve, and if in difficulty I think a small piece of meat could be placed at the end of each quarter to encourage the dog to quest. Finally, early training should take place on a field with only light cover.

F.H.: There is a difference in emphasis between training a spaniel and training a labrador. The trainer must not curb a

spaniel's drive and style, and more work is required in the
rabbit pen where game abounds. Spaniel pens are usually
larger than those required for retrievers – a spaniel is essen-
tially a hunting dog and on his ability to find game he must
be judged.

34. The dog who won't get into a car

PROBLEM: A puppy 6 months old, who is frightened of getting into a car either because of the noise of the vehicle or
because he is travel sick.

J.K.: Fear of a car may be present in a very nervous type
of dog – or it can be associated in a dog's mind with something unpleasant. The most usual cause is car sickness.
Many puppies are car sick the first time out in a car, and it
is usual to feed a puppy at the end of a journey and not
before. One adult dog I had was sick at exactly 30 miles –
he always showed reluctance to get into a car but was all
right around town and at local shoots. However, if a dog
persistently gets sick, he is really no use as a shooting dog.
If a dog is car-nervous, patience is the only cure. Feed him
in the car, let him sleep in the car. It may take a month
before he is willing to jump in, but he must never be forced
in. Prevention, however, is better than cure. Get the pup
used to the car and the noise of the engine before taking
him on a drive.

F.H.: The obvious thing to do is to make the association a
pleasant one. Sit in the car with the dog, talking and patting him; feed him. Also, have one or more dogs with you
in the car and he may forget what he is frightened of. If
the dog suffers from travel sickness, a pretty good and fairly
successful remedy is one of the brands of pills used for sea
sickness. I have used Kwells with success.

35. The handler who sends his dog away to be trained

PROBLEM: What type of owner sends his dog to a professional trainer?

J.K.: The shooting man sends his dog away to be trained, but he usually makes two mistakes: he doesn't realize how long it takes to train a dog properly – 9 months at least, and this he does not wish to afford – nor does he realize that unless he himself is trained, the dog will revert in a matter of days. If all he wishes is a dog that is pegged down at the covert side and will return on a whistle, he could quite well manage this himself.

F.H.: Then there are the amateurs who wish to run in trials but haven't the experience or time. There's no point in reading this book unless you train your own dog. Granted, you don't get the work but neither do you get the pleasure. I think that there is more enjoyment and satisfaction in training a dog to field-trial standards than there is in eventually running it in competitions. You don't need a lot of time – a little and often each day, possibly twenty minutes in a morning or evening. I don't think a dog someone else has trained ever really belongs to you. After all, the trainer is a man who asserts his will over the animal.

J.K.: Then there is the amateur trainer who sends his dog away to a professional in order that a fault may be cured. The owner knows the dog better than the professional and should know more about the fault and how to cure it. Also, if the professional does cure the fault, it is liable to return when the dog returns to the care of its master. A dog soon realizes when he gets back that his master has been changed. Moreover if the reader has read this chapter, he knows how to cure faults. So, having taken away the professional trainer's livelihood, Frank and I conclude the dialogue.

VIII

Working Tests and Retriever Field Trials

Working Tests

It is controversial whether working tests are good or bad for the future of field trials. They are good provided they are used as a means to an end, that is to train a trial dog; they are bad if they become an end in themselves – they mislead the handler as to the value of his dog and do harm to the breed.

The more members a Field Trial Society has, and the more people who are interested in trials or take part, the better. The day may come when the generous donors, who each year supply us with ground and who unselfishly give their time and are prepared to suffer the cold and wet while watching in some cases indifferent dogs, and who may not even possess a dog themselves, may become extinct. Should this happen – and in these days of syndicates finding ground becomes more and more difficult each year – societies may have to consider renting shoots themselves. This would be prohibitive in cost unless the society was very wealthy and had a lot of members. If working tests get more people into trials then working tests are worth while.

There are those who do not look upon working tests in this light. There was a suggestion from a society that the Kennel Club should recognize a working-test champion (God forbid! – having show champions is bad enough). Some people spend the whole of the summer going from one test to another – if the weather is good this can be a pleasant way of spending a Sunday, and provided the dog is a good marker and biddable, prizes will be won. However, a working test is *no* test of whether a dog is hard-mouthed, a squeaker, of whether he will run in under stress and not even of whether he is a good heeler under trial conditions. At a working test squeaking is seldom taken into account, hard mouth never.

A novice may see a particular dog winning at working tests and decide to breed from it or buy one of its pups. He trains the pup and spends a lot of time with it until it becomes quite a useful dog: he may even win some tests with it, and so decides to try the dog out at a field trial. Having paid the £5 entrance fee, travelled 200 miles or so and stayed the night at the H.Q. hotel, costing another £8, he goes to the trial, and on the first retrieve the judge examines the bird, shows it to the other judge and to our novice and throws him out of the trial. The novice may not even know what it is all about. There is no humour in this situation: the dog has committed the eliminating fault of squeezing the bird – a fault which is hereditary. If you breed from such a dog, although it may miss a generation, you are perpetuating the fault and it will crop up again. Handlers in the past have used hedgehog skins and pins in dummies and other weird and wonderful cures, but hard mouth is incurable. Whining likewise can be held in check for a season or two, but then gets out of hand and also has a hereditary factor.

A working test should be judged as far as possible like a field trial, and, for the last test, dead pigeons should be used to allow the judges to handle each bird and test for hard mouth. If a bird is squeezed, the dog should be eliminated.

Such a rule would lessen the chance of people buying puppies from such parents which in turn would help to eliminate the fault from the breed. Working tests must never be taken too seriously or considered as a substitute for field trials. They are a means but not an end in themselves.

Field Trials

The fairest way to run a trial would be for every dog to have the same type of bird in the same kind of cover, but even then, unless it was made artificial, some dogs would have a dead bird to collect while others would be sent on a runner. The element of luck cannot be eliminated in trials as they are conducted in this country, and there does not appear to be a better way in which they can be run. Most trials are run walking up in line through roots or on rough ground, with perhaps the occasional drive, and this is the best and most satisfactory way to judge dogs.

There are some grounds, most generously offered by hosts, that do not lend themselves to walking up game, and in these cases drives are the order of the day, which is most unsatisfactory, either to compete in or to judge.

Let us suppose that game is driven out of a wood over the guns and the shot birds drop in a patch of cover behind the guns. Now, from the first bird coming over the guns until the end of the drive, at least 10 to 15 minutes will have elapsed and at the end of the drive there may be a dozen birds down. With three judges you would have six dogs in line, and if the birds have been driven out at the end of the wood or a corner, then most of the birds will be lying behind the centre judge, so that when he sends the first dog out, the dog possibly has the choice of eight to nine birds and he would be a downright fool beast if he couldn't pick one. This applies to the next dog. In fact, they each get two retrieves, and this doesn't tell the judge very much apart from the fact that they will retrieve and have soft mouths. There are now four or five birds left, and of these it is quite possible that two guns have shot the same bird, unknown to each other, and also the first shot may have been a runner and that will have been down for half an hour or so. Surely it is unfair to penalize a dog for failing to pick a runner under these conditions. The fairest way in these circumstances is to use the dogs in line and pick four of the birds and leave the doubtful two to the 'picker up'.

First dog down failure

This is quite a controversial subject. Some judges are adamant that a dog who fails when he is the first on a runner must be penalized so hard that he has no possible chance of getting into the awards. In fact, when it does happen and these people hear about it, they think it criminal. This is not so, however. If in the course of a trial several dogs are tried on a runner and none is picked, then scent must be virtually non-existent, and under these conditions if every dog in the stake were tried first dog down, all would fail. So it seems hard to penalize a dog so heavily that he cannot get back into the stake when other dogs, possibly inferior, are put up merely because they have had the good fortune to have dead birds shot in front of them. If, on the other hand, some or even one dog in the stake has shown his ability to follow a line and pick a bird, then a dog failing under similar circumstances and at a similar time must be penalized. If one dog has the concentration to keep his head down and work out a 'line', then in my opinion he deserves great credit for; after all, you keep a dog to pick the birds you cannot pick, and a dog taking a line and coming back with a live bird is far superior to a dog going second and third dog down on a dead bird, when the judge knows exactly where the bird is and gives the information to the handlers. After all, that bird could be picked by the gun. First dog down failures and 'eye wipes' should be treated on their merits, and if the judges are practical men and women who train, run and shoot over their own dogs, they will do this, and so make for a happy and successful trial. When dealing with animals and Nature, any rules laid down must be flexible.

Drives

We have already mentioned the unfairness that can occur with this method of testing dogs, but it can be somewhat simplified. If a drive can be stopped when there are half a dozen birds down and the dogs in line used before the birds have been down too long, and then other dogs brought into the line, in this way all and not just a few of the dogs will be tested. It is better to treat all dogs as far as possible in the same manner and under the same conditions.

Another problem can arise here. If there are several birds down in a wood and dogs are sent in to work out of sight, then you never know from where the dog has picked a bird. One of the dogs under the centre judge may have hunted around and picked a bird which really belongs, say, to the right-hand judge. He then tries a dog on a bird which, unbeknown to him, has already been gathered, one being left lying in the middle. The dog may, of course, hunt around and find it, but if this is the last bird left, he will need quite a lot of time; and he is not likely to get too long so is going to be penalized for no fault of his own. Again, it is fairer to leave the last couple of birds to be picked up. One good thing about a drive is that it enables the judges to test the dogs for steadiness, to see that they sit quietly throughout the drive without making a noise, because a dog is more likely to squeak, if he is that way inclined, during the time he sits through a drive than when he is walking up.

How to become a Judge

Judging in field trials
When you enter your first trial, probably with some

trepidation, provided you have a decent dog and have trained it properly, you have taken your first step towards judging. It usually happens that after running for several years in trials up and down the country and meeting with a reasonable amount of success, some secretary will write to you on behalf of a Field Trial Society inviting you to judge, most probably a Novice Stake, in the company of one or perhaps two experienced judges. You feel quite pleased that you have been asked, but if you accept, as you should, then the doubts begin to arise, and surely there is good reason for them. Here you are in business or doing some full-time job, spending your spare time – and not all of that – 'playing with dogs'. Now in the near future you have to give your opinion of the ability of a dog which may possibly have been trained and is being handled by one of the top professionals! The top professional trainers in this country can hold their place anywhere in the world; they are not good, they are very good. You as a mere novice who has spent several years picking their brains and asking their advice, which they have always given most generously, are now in company with two others to sit in judgement on their dogs.

Prior to the fateful day you will receive word from the secretary of the Society which has been so foolhardy as to invite you, telling you that a room has been reserved for you at the Headquarters Hotel; and in the afternoon prior to the meet day you set out in the car for a four- or five-hour journey, beset by misgivings. You have now four hours or so to ponder all the things that can go wrong and the 101 mistakes that can so easily be made. You think of the times you have seen experienced judges make mistakes, so what chance have you? You wonder what the chances are of getting away after the trial so as to avoid being lynched, because there may be only one man on speaking terms with you when the day is over – the winner.

However, all things come to an end, even nightmare car

journeys, and you arrive at your destination, park the car, and think about feeding the dog and letting him have a run – then you realize that for the first time in years he isn't with you. It all depends on you. What a thought! You go to your room, take a bath and hope you will soon feel a little better; then you wander into the bar for a drink before dinner. The secretary will probably be there, and he or she will try to put you at ease. Your co-judges may also be there and you will undoubtedly know them – you will most likely have run a dog under them at some time – and so to dinner and then a few more drinks. Things begin to look a little brighter – what a wonderful difference a few drinks can make!

The fateful morning arrives and you wonder if the whisky of the night before was really a good idea. Boots and leggings on and coat donned, and the secretary gives you your judge's book, sometimes complete with pencil, which you lose anyway. Then you have a chat with your co-judges as to what position you take in the line. If you are judging with two 'A' judges, you will most likely go into the centre position, where one or both of the other judges will be able to keep an eye on you.

Your steward comes up to you and tells you he has Nos. 3 and 4 dogs for you, so you take your position in the line with No. 3 on the right and No. 4 on the left and a gun on the outside of each dog. You go over again in your mind the *Guide to Field Trial Judges* which you have read so many times since first being asked to officiate, and offer up a ritual prayer that you don't get confused between your left and your right. The steward of the beat raises his hand and you are on your own. Game comes to hand with regularity and you use the dog on your right first, then the dog on your left. If, however, the dog on the right side fails on a retrieve, the dog on the left is sent out. Then, as every dog should have a chance of a retrieve first dog down, the dog on the left is sent first for the next retrieve. When the first dog has had two retrieves, or the opportunity of two retrieves, your steward calls for another dog. You then move the dog already on your left to the right and put the new dog on your left so the next retrieve goes to the dog on the right, and the performance is repeated when the next new dog arrives. If scent is good and you have good dogs running you soon settle down and begin to enjoy the proceedings. Infinite pleasure can be got from watching a good dog doing his job well and in a polished fashion, regardless of who owns or handles him. So you carry on, breaking for lunch, until each dog has been down under two judges, probably having had two retrieves under the first judge and one retrieve on his second run. The judges then meet to have a consultation to compare notes on the merits of the dogs they have seen. These are usually classified as 'A' or 'B' or 'C' dogs, and the 'A' dogs are taken forward into the run-off. They are usually placed in the centre of the line under all three judges, with one judge giving the orders as to which dog retrieves. The order of retrieving at this stage is at the discretion of the judge, but he will try to protect his best dog or dogs, and they are more or less run off against each other.

Judges' Conference

Provided you have sufficient game, there is usually little doubt as to which is the winner. During the run-off you have the time, and indeed it is necessary, to look for the finer points of judging work: the way he hunts his ground, his speed, drive and perseverance; a clean, quick pick-up, fast return and a polished delivery; the way he answers the whistle and takes hand signals if looking for an unmarked bird – in fact, all those little things which, when put together, give you a 'polished' dog which is a joy to watch.

And so the day ends, the awards are read out by the secretary, the cups presented, probably by the owner of the ground or his wife, and then you wait in fear and trepidation for some handler to come and inquire as to your eyesight. Instead most of them come to you and shake your hand and thank you for the trouble you've taken, and as you journey home you realize that, after all the worry, it wasn't too bad. You have the satisfaction of knowing that you have given a little something back to the sport from which in the past you have taken so much, for if there were no judges, no generous donors of ground, there would be no field trials and thus would be lost a sporting atmosphere of comradeship, sportsmanship and light-hearted banter the like of which is not seen in any other pursuit or pastime.

Once you have been 'blooded' you will find yourself invited to judge other trials, be they Open or Novice Stakes, and soon some society will recommend to the Kennel Club that you be placed on the 'B' Panel of judges. The Kennel Club in their turn will inquire as to how many trials you have judged, which must be at least two, and will write to one of the senior judges with whom you have officiated asking for his observations as to your ability. Providing he has nothing derogatory to say, your name is then added to the list of 'B' judges. You carry on as before, running a dog, judging when you are asked, and when you have judged at two Open Stakes, you are eligible for recommendation to the 'A' Panel. Your name will then, sooner or later, be put forward to the Kennel Club, depending on the opinion of the Field Trial Secretary or the Society's judgement of your ability. A similar procedure ensues as for the 'B' Panel, and upon your elevation to 'A' judge, your name is removed from the list of 'B' judges and added to the list of 'A' judges. This list of judges, 'A' and 'B', is circulated to all Field Trial Societies to help them in their choice of judges for future events. The Committee of the Field Trial Society must know which judge is on the 'A' Panel because no field trial can be run without at least one 'A' judge officiating.

Once you are placed on the 'A' Panel, the weight of responsiblity can rest heavily upon your shoulders, because under the three-judge system at a Novice Stake, only the presence of one 'A' judge is necessary. It is possible, therefore to find yourself judging for the first time as an 'A' judge in the company of two judges who may never have judged before. Providing they are practical dog men of considerable experience, it doesn't matter much, but this is not always the case and you can find yourself with two co-judges who have had little practical experience of handling a dog, who appear never to have heard of *Kennel Club Rules* and obviously have not taken the trouble or time to read the *Guide to Field Trial Judges*, both of which are available from the Kennel Club and are also placed in the judges' notebook. In this event it is essential that you take up a position where you can see as much of the trial as possible, i.e. the centre, because in our experience the 'A' judge will be held responsible for any slip-up or mistakes made during the course of the day, whether he is directly involved or not.

General aspects of Judging

It is a pleasure to run under some judges, win or lose. Most of us are tensed up when we go in the line, wondering what our dogs are going to do, and a smile and a word from the judge does wonders to make the day enjoyable. Dr Berridge was one such judge. Once, when a dog was out, third dog down, the handler knew exactly where the partridge was – in fact, one more signal and he had picked it. The dog looked at him. He waved, nothing happened; he signalled again, nothing happened – then a loud voice from Dr Berridge behind him – 'That handler is so impatient he won't let his dog relieve himself . . .'

On another occasion the handler was doing well at a trial and was sent out first dog down to collect an easy pheasant in a wood. Every yard the dog took pheasants got up in all directions. By the time he had got her out the 30 yards necessary, the dog was so bewildered that she didn't know what she was doing. The handler was so confused he had forgotten where the pheasant was, so he was recalled. Dr Berridge said to him, more in sorrow than in anger, 'We don't train our dogs to run in aviaries, do we?'

Some judges are so strict and stick so rigidly to the rules that the handler feels that if he coughs he will be turned out. Now it is our contention that a dog should be judged by his overall performance, whether he is an 'A' dog or not. If a dog makes a slight noise as he yawns, he should not be turned out of the stake as a squeaker; if he heels rather in front of the handler, the handler should be allowed to speak to him and bring him back to heel. This is not to say that a persistently bad heeler should not be turned out of the trial, but the handler and the dog should be allowed to behave as they would on a normal shooting day. It always appears to me to be a bit artificial that a handler must not speak to his dog on a trial as he would if he was out shooting, and as for disturbing game, a quiet word to your dog makes for less disturbance than the conversation going on around you. In the same ways that training should be as positive as possible, so should judging. By the nature of field trials a lot of the dogs eliminate themselves and the judge is left with only a few dogs in the stake to judge, but this does not mean that a judge should try to eliminate dogs so that his work is made easier – this is a form of negative judging which should be condemned.

A judge, besides being pleasant and forgiving over minor faults and not sticking too rigidly to the rules, should also be a good marker. When the dog is out he really has little else to do except watch the dog and keep his mark on the bird. Although it is the handler's responsibility, it is extremely irritating to be told to hunt the wrong area and the judge must give his instructions plainly and take time to see that the handler understands them. A really gross abuse of this was when a judge said to a handler, 'There is a hare in the next field over that hedge. Send your dog.' The handler said, 'Where is the hare?' The judge said, 'I don't know, but send your dog out.' Well, the field was a very large one and the handler should have protested. However, he sent his dog. Not only was he tiring him out and curbing his enthusiasm, but the judge was learning nothing as he then turned to the other judge and started talking to him, presumably to find out where the hare was.

Judges can be very helpful, and it is their job to find out what the dog is worth, not whether the handler is a good marker. After all, in the shooting field there would be a discussion as to where the game lay. An instance of being a good judge is, for example, when a judge turns to you and says, 'It's a runner, send it quickly'; or as on another occasion, when the handler was hunting his dog third dog down without success, the judge said, 'I should bring it in if I were you. I think the bird is in the next parish, and so you are tiring your dog unnecessarily.' This is better than just giving the order, 'Bring your dog in.' A judge should, without interfering too much with the handler, tell him if he thinks he is hunting in the wrong area; on occasions a judge has said, 'Don't whistle, leave the dog and let him hunt,' when he has thought the dog was going right. So it is within the judge's province to help the handler to the best of his ability.

A discussion arose between three judges as to whether a dog who has been sent across water to collect should be penalized if he did not come back across water. One said he must, the other two agreed that if a dog had a pheasant in his mouth, they did not mind how he came back as long as he returned by a quick route, that they were not running obedience tests and that a dog should be allowed to use his intelligence; further, if it was mistakenly insisted upon that a dog must return by water, the dog could be trained to do so. The first judge was being too meticulous; the other two were judging on the performance of the dog.

At the same trial on the second day, a dog – first dog down – who failed to mark the fall of a runner, which was never picked, was sent out of the line very quickly, and rightly so. It was a reasonable mark and this was a failure in performance.

A really good judge should be always putting himself in the place of the handler and asking himself, 'If I was the handler, would I consider this a fair retrieve, or would I be content to be failed if the dog I am judging was my dog?'

Handlers' Conference

Most handlers are good sportsmen – it is no use criticizing the judge who has to make up his mind in a split second; there are so many decisions to make and luck plays such a great part in trials that most triallers learn to take the rough with the smooth. If the handler really feels he has had a bad deal, a quiet word with the judge over a glass of beer in the evening is permissible. Angry words at the trial show bad sportsmanship and are completely unallowable.

There are many great characters in the Field Trial world. Mrs Wormald is one of these. At the age of 84 she even ran her own dog in a trial. On one occasion, as the night was clement and there was no room at the inn, she slept in her van together with her Field Trial Champion, Banjo. Early the following morning the car park attendant decided to investigate and opened the car door and was immediately bitten by Banjo. His lamentations aroused Mrs Wormald from her sleep, but not deterred she addressed him as follows: 'Young man,' she said, 'what do you expect to happen if you open a lady's bedroom door without knocking?' The name of her present retriever is Boosey.

Another lady of Field Trial fame, and who is of rather magnificent proportions, was out duck shooting one early morning and was using a punt to collect the birds. However, she overbalanced and fell in the water with a great splash. Not dismayed, and spying a duck floating on the water a little way off, she thrashed her way towards it, grabbed it in her mouth and swam back to the punt. As she was hauled on board, she remarked, 'Well, how was that for a retrieve?'

This is the kind of spirit we need in our trials.

The Three-Judge System

To run an Open Stake a society must have at least two 'A' judges. For a Novice Stake, only one 'A' judge is required. A Novice Stake is usually but not always run with three judges, which means that each dog, unless it commands an eliminating fault, must go under two judges. The procedure is more often than not that you get two retrieves, or the opportunity of two retrieves under your first judge, and then one retrieve under your second judge. In this way a fair amount of game is conserved which can be used for dogs which are left in for the run-off. To explain this a little more clearly: when a dog goes under a judge the first time he is given the chance of the first retrieve. Should he be successful, the next retrieve is given to the dog on the judge's left, i.e. No. 2. If he does the job properly the next bird is given to No. 1. Should he meet with success he then goes out of the line and another dog is called in. The No. 2 dog then goes to the right of the judge, because he has the next retrieve, and the new dog, say No. 7, goes on the left – in this way each dog has its chance of an 'eye-wipe' over his neighbour, i.e. if No. 1 is sent for a bird and he fails, then No. 2 is tried and if he succeeds he becomes No. 1, and has the first opportunity to retrieve. The next bird down is given to No. 2, and so it proceeds until all the dogs have had two retrieves under one of the judges. The time is now due for the judges to have a conference and compare notes as to the quality of the various dogs: an odd one may have 'run in' so he is eliminated, another one may have gone out of control – if this is the opinion of two judges, he also is eliminated. Also any dog guilty of squeezing a bird, provided all the judges have examined the game, also departs. All the dogs now left have to run under a different judge from the one who saw them previously. Usually they get just one retrieve. The second time through is relatively quicker than the first time. It can depend, of course, on how many dogs are left from the first round.

The judges now have another duty – this is more revealing, for now two judges have seen each dog, one in the first round and the other in the second, so they are both in a position to discuss each dog's ability – marking, retrieving, hunting, heeling, and in general to assess how polished his performance is. From this conference the outstanding dogs are sorted out, possibly three, four or five, and they are taken into the centre of the line under all three judges for the run-off. If a dog has been outstanding during the trial it may well be left out as the winner – it is the reserved dog – and the remainder run off for second, third and fourth places. But it would be quite an easy and not very convincing win if it had only had three retrieves, unless, of course, the retrieves had consisted of very strong runners, or it had been sent third and fourth dog down and would, therefore, have wiped the eye of over half the dogs in the stake.

For a Novice Stake, the three-judge system is the best, for it gives newcomers a chance of three retrieves and therefore gives both the handler and the dog some experience, as against running under four judges with its sudden death. Although no dog doing badly on his first two retrieves would have much chance of figuring in the awards, it at least gives a beginner the chance of going into the line again, and perhaps he may profit from any mistakes he may have made during his first run.

There is another point in favour of three judges: some dogs are a bit slow to get going and some are rather excited when they first go into the line, and in their first run rate a 'B' qualification; yet, under the next judge, the dog may be really brilliant, and can possibly go on to get into the money. Under four judges this is very unlikely to happen because a dog having its first two retrieves has already been seen by two judges, and, if it has behaved in an unworkmanlike fashion, it would be discarded; this is a pity because the object of the judges is to try to the best of their ability to find the best dog on the day and not to look for faults in order to discard dogs and so lessen the field. This is a very strong argument in favour of the three-judge system. It is probably fairer to the handler to run under the four-judge system, but from the judges' point of view it is preferable to only have three.

The Four-Judge System

In this case the judges work in two pairs, but at least one of each pair must be on the 'A' Panel. This system has an advantage over the three-judge system, in so far as there is less likelihood of two judges making the same mistakes at the same time: dogs are less likely to be sent out in the wrong order, which can be very important if there is a strong runner down and the judges are working on the theory that a 'first dog down' failure is out of the stake, regardless of whether or not the bird is picked. Another point is that if one judge has a leaning towards a certain handler or a particular dog, then he must try to convince his co-judge. Provided his co-judge is an honest man and has some courage, he will need to put forward a pretty convincing argument, otherwise his opinion against three other judges will not carry much weight.

The four-judge system also helps to conserve game because, if a dog has failed miserably on his first run, he does not need to go in the line again before being discarded, as he will have already been under two judges, and this rule can save quite a lot of game in a 24-dog stake.

In the course of a trial there often crops up some unique problem, one which makes you doubtful as to the right decision to make. You don't have the advantage of sitting over a pint of beer with two or three experienced handlers and judges and discussing the pros and cons at length; you have to give a decision there and then, and it could be an advantage to discuss it for a couple of minutes with your co-judge. It is often said that 'two heads are better than one'; it is also said that 'too many cooks spoil the broth', so you pay your money and then take your choice. We are, after all, engaged in a sport, so if you don't like a particular system, or you object to the judge, you don't have to run your dog; there is no one forcing you to run in any particular trial.

Difficult Decisions and a Quiz on Judging

During several years of trialling both as competitors and as judges, quite a few problems have arisen, and even now we still go over in our minds decisions we made years ago and wonder if we did the right things. Quite often a situation arises in which one has had no previous experience and there are only a few minutes in which to make a judgement. It is of great importance to the competitor that the decision should be right even though they (the competitors) do not always agree.

At a trial on one occasion we went into a field of roots. A bird was shot about 40 yards out to the right-hand dog, and that dog was duly sent out for its first retrieve. About 15 yards from the handler it came across a dead bird, evidently one which had been shot previously, had carried on and dropped in this particular field unseen by anyone. The dog picked it and brought it to the handler. The bird was taken from him and the dog again dispatched for the original bird. On completing this retrieve the handler took out his lead and asked if he had finished. He was told to stay in the line and the left-hand dog was sent for the next bird. Then the right-hand dog was sent again. After this retrieve he was told to put his lead on. The handler showed his displeasure at lunchtime and claimed he was unfairly given three retrieves against other competitors having the normal two.

There may be people who would agree with the handler's view, but if the problem is looked at more closely, there is another and surely better solution. If the judge had happened to see the dead bird, which the dog first picked, and the dog had not retrieved it, he could be thought guilty of 'blinking' the bird. The dog's job is to pick dead or wounded game, so the animal was quite right. On being sent for the bird which was shot in front of him, which the handler claimed was his second retrieve, had he failed on this bird then the left-hand dog would have been sent and he would have had the chance of an 'eye-wipe', so it was proper to keep the right-hand dog in the line so that it would have the same opportunity for an 'eye-wipe' if the left-hand dog had failed on his first bird. The handler would have had a legitimate complaint had he been sent out of the line after the first two retrieves, even though one was accidental, and then when a new dog was called in the new dog had the opportunity of going second dog down on what might be a comparatively simple bird. The point is that if No. 1 dog fails, and No. 2 dog has the opportunity of an eye-wipe', then to be fair, if No. 2 dog fails, No. 1 dog should have the chance of going behind him, and in this way both dogs are given pretty much the same chance against each other, and this should continue throughout the trial.

However, in the case of a dog drawn No. 12 in a 12-dog stake or No. 24 in a 24-dog stake, this does not always happen. In the *Kennel Club's General Regulations for the Conduct of Field Trials* it states that no dog *shall be called up* for a trial a second time until every dog in the stake has been tried once. This means that quite often a dog is left in line on his own, which is most unfair. The last dog is generally brought to the centre of the line, but a bird may be shot anywhere, and the very best he can hope for is to 'keep his nose clean'. Apart from picking a good runner, he is on a 'hiding to nothing'. The second time through the card this cannot be avoided, but it need not happen the first time. If the wording of the *Regulations* was modified as follows: 'No dog may be tried a second time until every dog has been tried once', then No. 1 dog would be called up into the line with No. 12, but No. 12 would get its first retrieve and would have the chance of going behind No. 1 dog should he fail on a bird.

When a bird is down and is known to have run, and a dog follows the line, coming back without the bird, it is always important, if at all possible, to examine the area where the dog has lost the bird. On one occasion a bird had run and then fallen into a drain almost 8 feet deep and 2 feet wide. The only way a dog could have got it was to have fallen in, and he couldn't possibly have scrambled out again. In effect, the bird was unpickable and the dog was given due credit for a good mark and for following the line until the bird disappeared – he couldn't have done more.

There are occasions when birds are left, and then a 'picker-up' is called up to try to find the bird. Normally when a picker-up is called in the judge has finished with that retrieve, and he judges the dogs he has tried on the ability they have shown, the first dog tried being the one most heavily penalized because, after all, he had the best chance. There are some judges, however, who if the picker-up is successful, then discard the dogs who have failed. If this happened throughout the whole of the trial, at least each dog failing would be treated the same, but these judges do not appear to follow a pattern. Some dogs are put out and some are left in – a most confusing situation for anyone trying to follow what is going on, and most unfair. In fact, the use of a picker-up to put dogs out is definitely wrong. It is one thing to handle a dog from 40 yards away and not be too sure exactly where the fall is while having a limited amount of time; it is very different to walk about in the area where the bird fell, sending one or two dogs in front of you, looking for the feathers to mark the fall and having all the time in the world at your disposal. There is no comparison.

Here is another problem which a judge may have to face. A dog is sent out for a bird, makes a find, goes in to pick it, and the bird flies away low over the ground. The dog chases the bird, his handler whistles and tries to stop him, but fails. The dog eventually catches the bird and comes back with it. Now, had the bird run instead of flown, the handler would most probably have done nothing, the dog would have caught the bird and, if he had behaved in the same way as when the bird flew, then he would have been credited with a retrieve and that would have been the end of it. But, once he had made

an unsuccessful attempt to stop it, then he left the way open
to doubts. The dog did not obey the whistle and therefore it
could be said that he ran in or was out of control. Had the
dog stopped to the whistle, then he would either have been
recalled or sent on after the bird at the judge's discretion, but
in any case the handler would have demonstrated his dog's
obedience, and that would have done him no harm when the
judges were going through their books. A case such as this
must be judged on its merits, and account taken of the hap-
penings at that particular time, but broadly speaking in this
case the dog was disobedient and should have been heavily
penalized, if not discarded completely. Whichever decision a
judge makes it would be open to argument and undoubtedly
cause some controversy among the handlers.

A quiz on judging

The following examples have all occurred at field trials. It
may interest the reader to make his own decision before
reading the answers.

Question 1: A judge sends out the wrong dog on a runner,
which is never picked subsequently. The dog is therefore a
first dog down failure. How is he judged?

Answer: The judge has made an honest mistake. This is bad
luck on the handler, but the dog must be judged on his
work.

Question 2: A wing-tipped pheasant falls a long way off in a
small spinney, surrounded by barbed wire and a high fence.
Twenty minutes later, after the trial has reached the spinney, the bird is given to one of the handlers who refuses to
take it because of the wire. The judge then gives it to his
other dog, having taken him round to a more favourable
position. The pheasant is never picked. The handler who

refused the retrieve is carried on into the run-off, the other handler is discarded.

Answer: This is very bad judging. The retrieve should have been scrapped and the bird picked by the pickers-up. In any case, it is quite unjust to penalize a dog who has tried against a dog who was not allowed to go out.

Question 3: A runner falls in full view and makes off across an open field. A dog is sent immediately and there is an exciting and prolonged chase before the bird is brought to hand. The dog, a steady one, runs in at the next bird which falls in front of him. Should the judge have waited until the bird was out of sight? (It was an Open Stake).

Answer: It would be preferable to let the bird get to near-by cover before sending the dog. He would then lose sight of the bird but be near enough to get on the line and would have to use his nose. There would be a good chance of gathering the bird and less chance of unsteadying the dog. If the dog failed to pick it, it would be fair to penalize him as a first dog down failure. Most handlers would prefer to be put out for a first dog down failure than have an unsteady dog.

Question 4: A dog is sent out to a marked retrieve and quite obvious runner. The dog goes out to the fall very slowly, follows the runner about 30 yards and then loses it. How should he be judged?

Answer: This is a 'B' dog because he went out very slowly on an easy mark. Although he did make a reasonable job of following the track when he got there, he should be discarded.

Question 5: There is no scent and no runners are picked during the course of the trial. How do you judge the first dog down failures?

Answer: This, of course, depends on the amount of game and

the performance of other dogs. No dog should be automatically discarded. Each dog should be judged on the effort he makes and, while one could be discarded (see question 4), another could be carried forward.

Question 6: At a 'run-off', the dog who eventually is given second place in the trial, although not having an actual failure, puts up a very poor performance. The dog who comes third has two very good retrieves. Is this good judging?

Answer: All dogs in the run-off are presumably 'A' dogs. While it is correct judging for a 'reserved' dog to be sheltered up to a point, the dogs must be judged on their ability throughout the whole day. If in the run-off another dog shows brilliant form and does some good work, it is only fair that he be given a chance to win. Run, say, the two best dogs together and let them settle the order themselves.

Question 7: A dog who has done reasonable work in the morning is carried on into the afternoon as a 'B' dog. Apart from sitting at a 'stand' to demonstrate steadiness he is not given another retrieve though there was adequate game.

Answer: It is our contention that any dog who is carried on, either from the morning to the afternoon, or from one day to the next in a two-day stake, should have the opportunity, however small, of pulling himself up and being among the winners. The dog should certainly have been given a retrieve in the afternoon. Some dogs improve to a remarkable degree after they have settled down.

Question 8: In the run-off there are three dogs, and two pheasants down. It is unlikely that further birds will be shot. One dog is sent out and fails. A second dog collects it. The 'reserve' dog is not sent out on a retrieve. The judge then sends out the successful dog to collect the second pheasant.

Answer: This is bad judging. The dog who has a second dog down success and is then sent again is getting more retrieves than the eventual winner (the reserved dog). In any case, the dog who had wiped the eye of another dog in the run-off should have had a chance at the dog who was evidently 'on ice'. There does not seem to be any reason for sending this successful dog out again. The judge might have sent the reserve dog out – if he picked it then he wins and the number of retrieves has been evened out. Had he failed, then the other dog could have been tried and if successful would have been a worthy winner with two 'eye-wipes' to his credit. If both dogs had failed because the bird had run, then the first dog down would not be penalized because he would have been waiting while the other two dogs were tried with the first bird, but in this case they would be judged on their performance.

Question 9: A dog in roots causes a commotion by chasing a rabbit about 3 to 4 yards. The judge comes over, but by this time the dog is at heel. The handler did not speak to the dog. The judge ignored the incident.

Answer: This must depend on what the judge actually saw. However, it was a chase and the dog was not steady at heel and so the dog should have been discarded if it was an Open Stake.

Question 10: A dog at a stand is quite steady until the handler moves, then the dog thinks he is going to be sent out to a pheasant which has fallen 10 yards in front of him. The handler hisses and the dog freezes.

Answer: This is debatable. If you hiss at your dog it is the same as speaking to it. As in all things, you get punished not for what you do but for what you are caught doing.

While a low hiss is not audible like the spoken word, if the rest of the dogs had sat quietly, regardless of temptation, in fairness to others he should be penalized – the severity depending on how far he transgressed.

Question 11: A dog is sent out to a wounded hare which is kicking and squealing. The dog refuses to pick the hare. The judge tells the handler to pull back his dog and tells the gun to shoot the hare. However, the hare lies still and is thought to be dead. The handler sends his dog again. The hare starts struggling again. The dog, however, now collects the hare and retrieves it back to his master.

Answer: If this is an Open Stake the dog should be discarded. In a Novice Stake the dog should not have been sent out.

Question 12: A dog is sent out on a bird in a wood and is handled correctly into the area given by the judge. The gun then comes up and says the pheasant fell in a different area. The judge moves the dog and tells the handler this is his final cast.

Answer: As the dog had been sent into the wrong area, the first part of the retrieve should have been forgotten and the handler given adequate time. A similar incident occurred when a dog was working among bullocks. The judge asked the beaters to drive off the bullocks and in this case allowed the dog adequate time to work undisturbed.

Question 13: A pheasant falls in a wood. A dog is sent out from a fair distance away from the wood. When the dog enters the wood the handler is called forward so that he can direct his dog while it is working in the wood.

Answer: Correct. A judge should always try to put himself in the position of the handler and not make the retrieves too difficult. It is admitted that in this case the dog should have marked sufficiently well to have some idea where the pheasant had fallen.

Question 14: A hare is shot at on the left of the line, runs down the line and enters a wood. A beater reports that the hare is lying dead 25 yards inside the wood. The judge on the right-hand side of the line tells the beater to collect it.
Answer: It was the first morning of the trial and the dogs are only sent for game shot by their own guns.

Question 15: At the end of a drive all birds had been picked save one – a hen pheasant. Handlers were given a good mark and five dogs failed. The sixth dog was tried and went out at right angles to the handler, disturbed a rabbit and took a line down into the wood in spite of whistles and shouts. He eventually came back with a dead cock, picked at least 100 yards from where the other dogs had hunted. The first five dogs were put out of the trial and the sixth was kept in.
Answer: Either the judge had been given a bad mark, or more likely the hen had been picked previously. The cock had probably carried on and dropped dead. As you cannot penalize a dog for failing to pick what is not there, all five dogs should have been left in the stake. The fate of the sixth dog is debatable – he was out of control and although he was carried on he should have been severely penalized.

Question 16: A dog goes second dog down on a bird in a hole under a bank. In view of the judge and the handler the dog has to scratch a hole before he can get a grip on the bird. When he has pulled the bird out he takes another hold and the bird goes in again. The dog makes another try and this time is successful. One side of the bird was 'in' – the dog was put out of the stake.
Answer: This is very harsh judging. Under the circumstances

the dog should have been given another chance. It is unfair to condemn him to 'hard mouth' on that evidence.

Question 17: At a Novice Stake the dogs on the right of the line were waiting while a dog on the left was looking for a bird. A rabbit came down the line and ran into a dog sat besides its handler. The dog jumped, either in fear or surprise. The judge told him to put his lead on as his dog was unsteady.

Answer: A ridiculous decision, which makes you wonder why you travel over half the country and pay not inconsiderable expenses when you get this kind of judging.

Question 18: On one occasion at an Open Stake four dogs were tried on a bird and all failed. The bird was handpicked. The dogs were put out of the stake. Later in the day one dog was taken back and came third in the awards.

Answer: Even worse judging than in No. 17. I feel sure that dogs must be eliminated when a judge can hand-pick a bird in fairly light cover – which four dogs have failed to find. For one of the dogs to figure in the awards must be bad judging.

Question 19: A dog goes out of control in an Open Stake. The handler is sent out to gather his dog, which he does. He goes on to win the stake.

Answer: In the *Kennel Club Field Trial Rules*, if a dog is out of control it is an eliminating fault, provided the judges agree that it is out of control. The judges must have failed to agree in this instance although it is virtually impossible to put forward an argument in favour of a man who has walked out to collect his dog.

Question 20: In a trial run under the three-judge system, during the morning of the first day a dog was tried on a bird and failed. The judge tried his other dog, which also failed. He should then have asked his co-judges to try their dogs; instead he brought a dog out from among the spectators who found the bird.

Answer: In the *Guide to Field Trial Judges* it states that dogs should not be called into the line to look for a bird until all the dogs in the line have been tried. In this case the dog called in was successful but, had it not been, the unfortunate handler would have rightly been very upset. On the other hand, the dogs already in line had the opportunity of at least a third dog down success taken away from them – the other handlers were not very pleased. Their dogs would have had a better chance of finding the bird than one brought in, as they were already in the line, and if one of them had succeeded it may have made all the difference to the result of the trial.

POSTSCRIPT

...*It All Depends on the Dog*

'When he falls short, 'tis Nature's fault alone.
When he succeeds, the merit's all his own.'

In this book we have tried to solve some of the many problems that arise in the training of dogs. Perhaps we have attempted the impossible – most books tell you how to train but not what to do when the dog has other ideas. Even the attempt, however, makes one realize the extent of the problems that face the trainer.

We hope that the book will have given our readers food for thought and have enabled them to work out a programme when faced with the peculiarities of their own dogs.

As we said in the Preface, most of us are not able to make a choice from many dogs, but are stuck with the dog we have and by perseverance achieve a civilized animal, capable of giving us pleasure, doing his job satisfactorily and winning the occasional trial. We do feel, however, that there is probably too much indiscriminate breeding. It is no use mating a brash animal with a too biddable one in the hope that the result will be somewhere between the two extremes – the probability is that the result will still be some biddable puppies and some brash ones. Nature does not average out. It is far better and cheaper in the long run to buy a pup from a professional which is line-bred to a dog or bitch that has really proved itself than to breed from an animal of no great talent that one happens to possess. Very few of us have the time or opportunity to establish a true line. However hard a trainer works, it is impossible to produce a polished dog out of poor material. So, in the final outcome, it all depends on the dog.

In the same manner as there are too many haphazardly bred dogs (we are not saying badly bred dogs), there are too many people who don't understand how a dog's mind works, and we have tried to correct this. Although a mind is a very complex machine, the actual mechanics of its working are relatively simple and can be analysed to a few simple factors, such as instincts, associations, emotions and urges – which are a combination of instincts and emotions. Although each dog has an individual over-riding temperament, it should be possible to plan a course of training to correct this and to predict the result of any course of action. Trying to get into the mind of a dog is well worth while and is a fascinating exercise even if there are no practical results. In fact there usually are, as we hope we have shown.

A book cannot teach anybody to train a dog – a dog has to be handled and some people find it difficult to acquire the necessary skill. The horse rider talks of 'good hands' and 'gentling a horse'. The term 'handling a dog' seems to mean something different. The good handler knows how to gentle his dogs because, through his touch, he can communicate with them. A strange dog should be allowed to approach you in his own time; but if you wish to approach a dog quickly, you should move the back of your hand towards him from below (because in dog language all menace comes from above – even his mother's teeth snap down from above the puppy).

Other people will try out a training exercise and discard it because the dog does not conform; they have not the patience and perseverance that they require of their dogs. A lesson to be well and truly taught takes a week or two. A fault to be permanently eradicated takes at least a month; some faults are only suppressed and have the annoying habit of raising their ugly heads just when the trainer thinks he has succeeded and can pass on to other things.

But in training there is more true knowledge and fascination than ever came from shooting a bird dead in the air, although each has its part and its skills.

It may be apparent in these pages that we like different types of animals. One of us (Frank Haworth) likes a fast, good-going dog as long as it is biddable – because this type of animal has style and covers more ground. The other (J. A. Kersley) likes a biddable dog as long as it is fast because this type of animal is more easily trained and is nearer what the shooting man requires, and after all, we train and breed for shooting. So, paradoxically, we are very near yet poles apart. We have wondered, if we changed over, how we would get on and whether our results would be the same. We are sure that each trainer should stick to the type of animal he likes and to which he is best suited.

No one can deny that the selective breeding and advanced training given to Field Trial dogs improves the breed. However, we may also be breeding a race of over-trained and rather useless dogs. The keeper and beater do not really want a field trial dog – they want a dog which will work in front of them and they can always walk over to pick a bird; they work their dogs near to them. The formal shooter probably does not need a dog at all, as his birds can be picked either by himself or by the beaters. If possessing a dog gives him pleasure or prestige, he wants a quiet animal that he does not have to manage or keep in training. The rough shooter would rather take crossbred Jack Russell on a shoot than his field trial animal, unless there are other dogs to put up the game. Without the other dogs he could walk all day and never see a bird. All of us, however, need a disciplined animal over which we have control, and this at least we produce.

If we had our time over again, we perhaps might prefer to train springers or pointers, except that the latter are not over-blessed with brains; or perhaps we would have a Coon Hound and follow long trails. In that case we would probably have to own a horse. On second thoughts, we would stick to retrievers – we love our trial dogs because they give us an all-the-year-round occupation and amusement; because we get to know them intimately; and because we believe they are, of all shoot-ing dogs, the most intelligent and interesting. We enjoy the competition of trials and the good fellowship of triallers, because – there being no monetary gains – trials are a sport in the true sense of the word, and between trials we can go shooting and collect the game that others cannot get.

If you read old books on training written at the end of the last and the beginning of this century, you will find that direction signals were at that time almost non-existent, but the dogs were trained to hunt endlessly, go through sludge and slush, swim estuaries and fast-flowing rivers and not to come back without the bird – after all, their master's evening meal and perhaps his livelihood depended upon it. And one wonders to what extent we have erred in our present-day training. Conditions have altered; now it is mainly a question of field trials and formal shoots. But one cannot help harking back to the past, to the really rough shooting which our true wild-fowler experiences today, to shooting (of which we have memories) on the estuary in the dark when it all depended on the dog, whether he brought back the duck or not, and this was very important. 'Irrational', did I say? In the words Nicholas Cox might have used: 'There must always be a place for an honest dog, in plain English.'

Index